NELSON BEATS THE ODDS

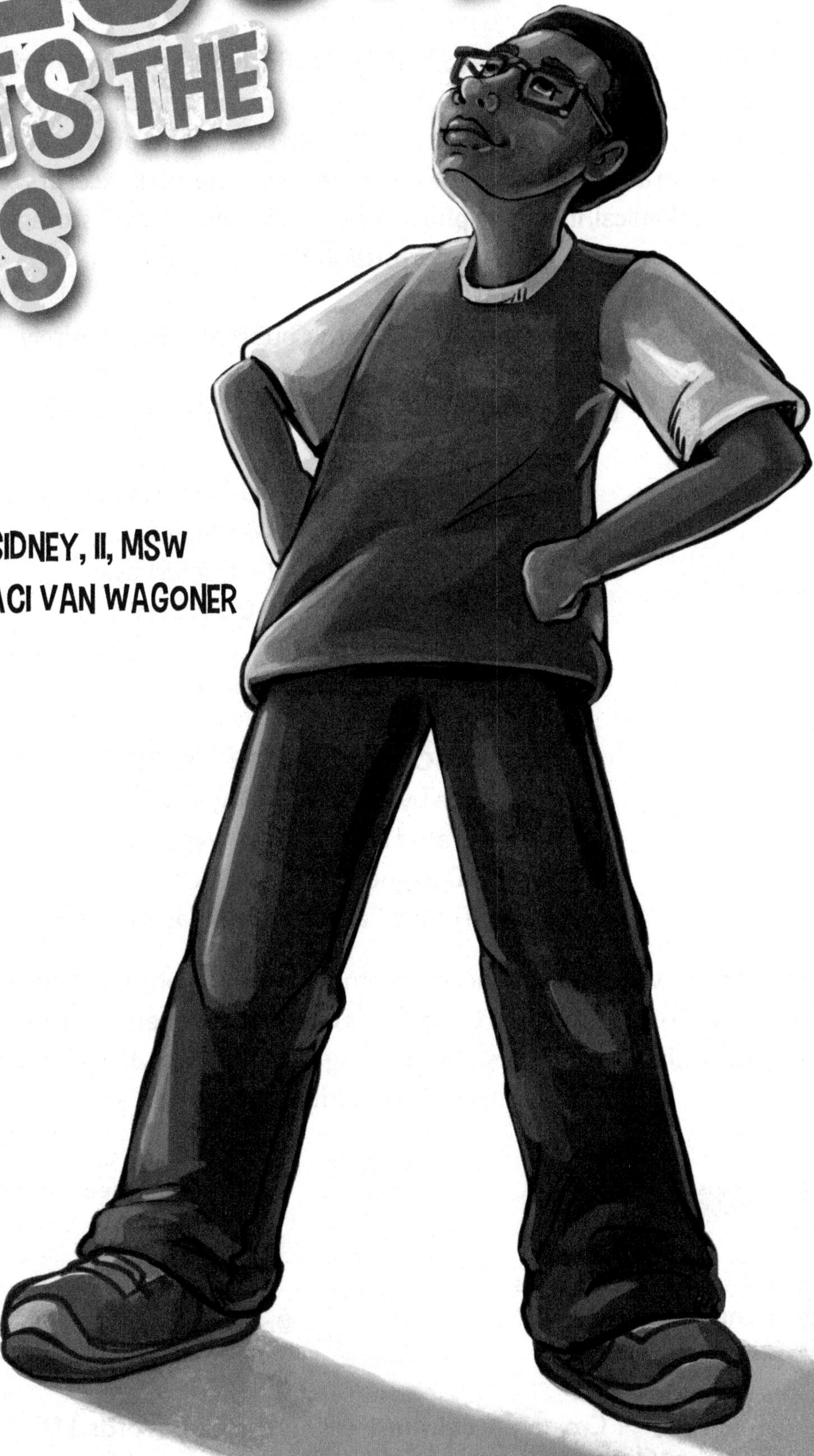

WRITTEN BY: RONNIE SIDNEY, II, MSW
ILLUSTRATED BY : TRACI VAN WAGONER

NELSON BEATS THE ODDS. Second Printing.

Published by Creative Medicine: Healing Through Words,
P.O. Box 2749, Tappahannock, VA, 22560

Library of Congress Control Number: 2015912475

ISBN 978-0-9965324-1-9 (hard cover)
ISBN 978-0-9965324-3-3 (paperback)
ISBN 978-0-9965324-2-6 (paperback)
ISBN 978-0-9965324-0-2 (ebook)

PRINTED IN THE USA

Nelson Beats the Odds

Written by: Ronnie Sidney, II, MSW
Illustrated by: Traci Van Wagoner
Designed by: Kurt Keller
Edited by: Tiffany Carey Day and Katrina Kiefer

Please visit www.nelsonbeatstheodds.com for information about Nelson Beats the Odds, Tameka's New Dress, Nelson Beats the Odds Comic Creator app, teacher's guide and mixtap Follow us on social media and use the hashtag #TamekasNewDress, #NelsonBeatsTheOdds #NBTO and #iBeatTheOdds.

 @nelsonbeatstheo

 @nelsonbeatstheo   @ronniesidneyii

 Nelson Beats The Odds
Ronnie Sidney, II, MSW
#iBeatTheOdds

 @nelsonbeatstheo   @ronniesidneyii

Creative Medicine: Healing Through Words, LLC

This awesome undertaking would not have been possible without Imagine That! Design. Thank you for bringing my story to life and providing quality service. Special thanks to my editors, Tiffany Carey Day and Katrina Kiefer, for reviewing my project.

To the loves of my life, Talisha, Mali and Morgan, thank you all for your patience and love.

To my beautiful and supportive family: Ronnie Sidney, Sr., Gwendolyn Sidney, Cherlanda Sidney-Ross, Van Ross, Deandre Sidney, Sydney Ross, Endia Ross, Robert Patrick, Sarah Harris, Etta Wright and Gail Wright.

To some very special individuals and organizations: Ruth E Tobey; Essex County Public Schools; MP-NNCSB; Dr. Nicki Lee; Karla Luster; Mi Casa Fitness; Derek Hence; Michelle Matthews; Fredericksburg DSS; Cathleen Newbanks; Anne Holton, Virginia Secretary of Education; FACES of Virginia Families; National Foster Care Association; Good Hope Baptist Church; VCU Medical Center's IVPP; Richmond Association of Black Social Workers; NABSW; NASW; The Fatherhood Takeover; Anita Latane; Joseph Taylor; Luxe Lengths; Bundy family; Rich family; Johnson family; Boyd George; Shawn Long; Christopher Pitts; Larry Brayboy; Del Potter; Rena Shipp; Lashari Wright; Katie Mazeika; Jazmine Campbell.

In closing, I wish to dedicate this book to the memory of Teddy Rich and Arthur "Maine" Bundy.

CREATIVE MEDICINE
HEALING THROUGH WORDS

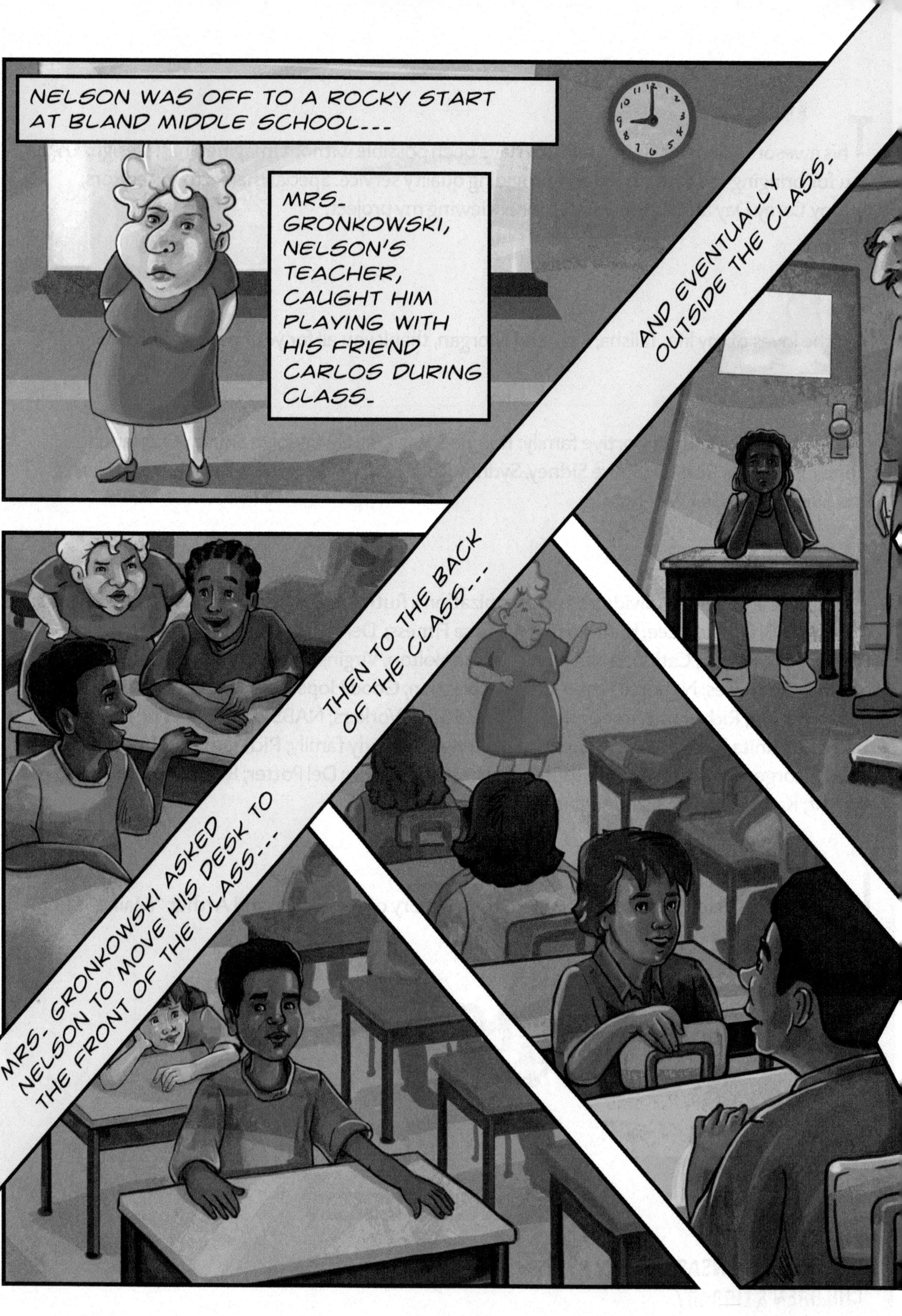

NELSON WAS OFF TO A ROCKY START AT BLAND MIDDLE SCHOOL...
MRS. GRONKOWSKI, NELSON'S TEACHER, CAUGHT HIM PLAYING WITH HIS FRIEND CARLOS DURING CLASS.
MRS. GRONKOWSKI ASKED NELSON TO MOVE HIS DESK TO THE FRONT OF THE CLASS...
THEN TO THE BACK OF THE CLASS...
AND EVENTUALLY OUTSIDE THE CLASS.

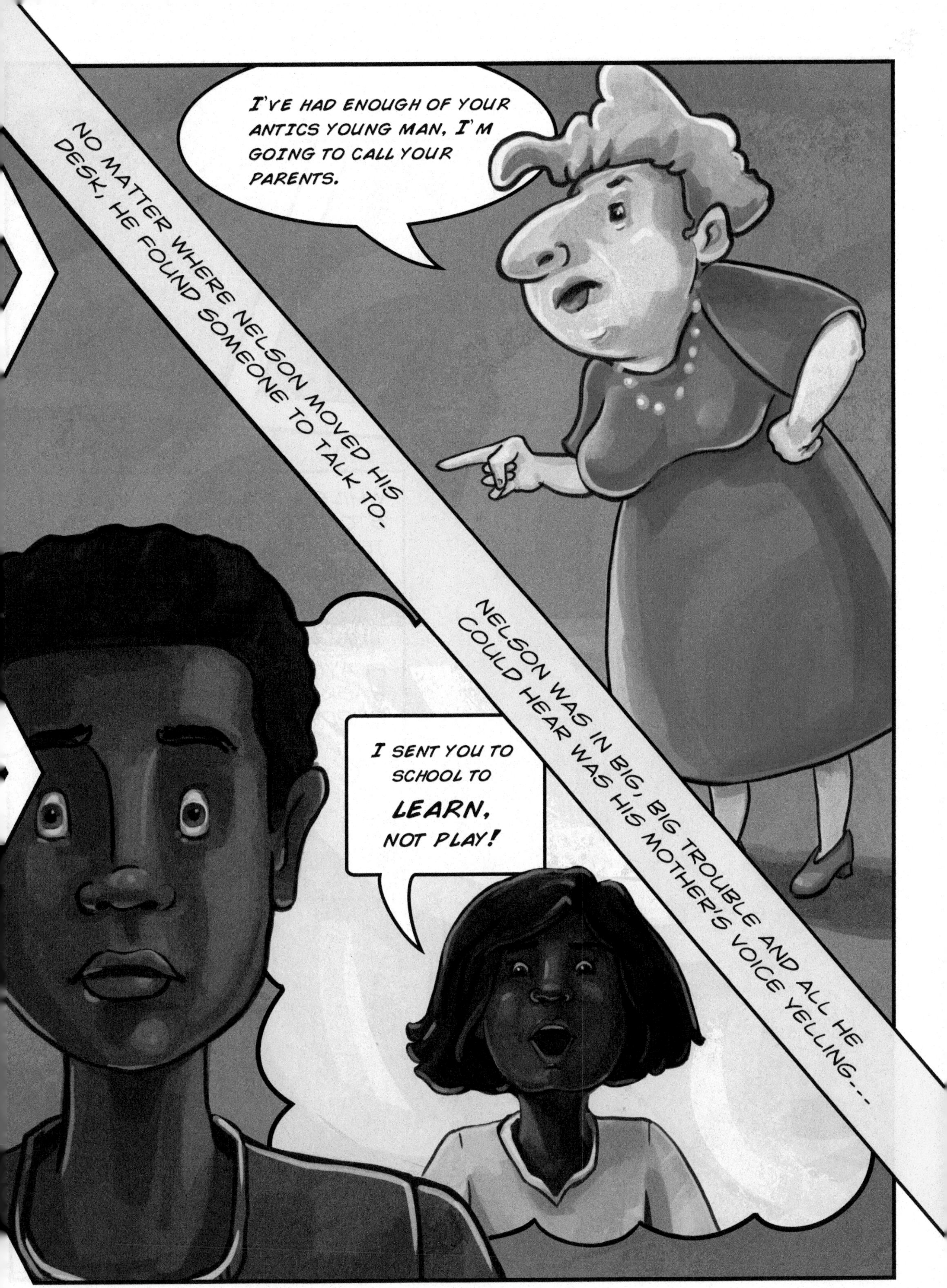

NO MATTER WHERE NELSON MOVED HIS DESK, HE FOUND SOMEONE TO TALK TO.
I'VE HAD ENOUGH OF YOUR ANTICS YOUNG MAN, I'M GOING TO CALL YOUR PARENTS.
NELSON WAS IN BIG, BIG TROUBLE AND ALL HE COULD HEAR WAS HIS MOTHER'S VOICE YELLING...
I SENT YOU TO SCHOOL TO LEARN, NOT PLAY!

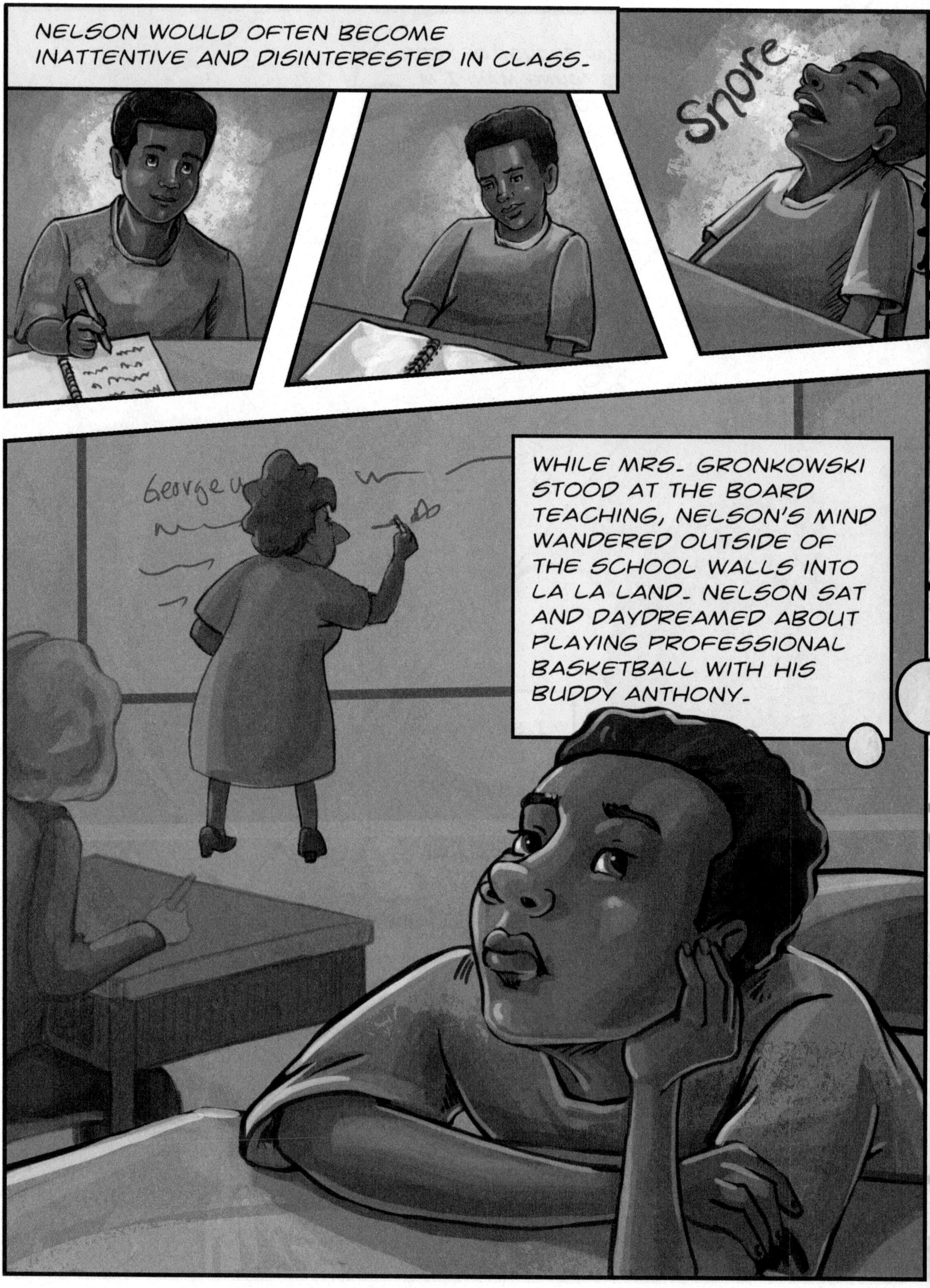
NELSON WOULD OFTEN BECOME INATTENTIVE AND DISINTERESTED IN CLASS.
Snore
WHILE MRS. GRONKOWSKI STOOD AT THE BOARD TEACHING, NELSON'S MIND WANDERED OUTSIDE OF THE SCHOOL WALLS INTO LA LA LAND. NELSON SAT AND DAYDREAMED ABOUT PLAYING PROFESSIONAL BASKETBALL WITH HIS BUDDY ANTHONY.

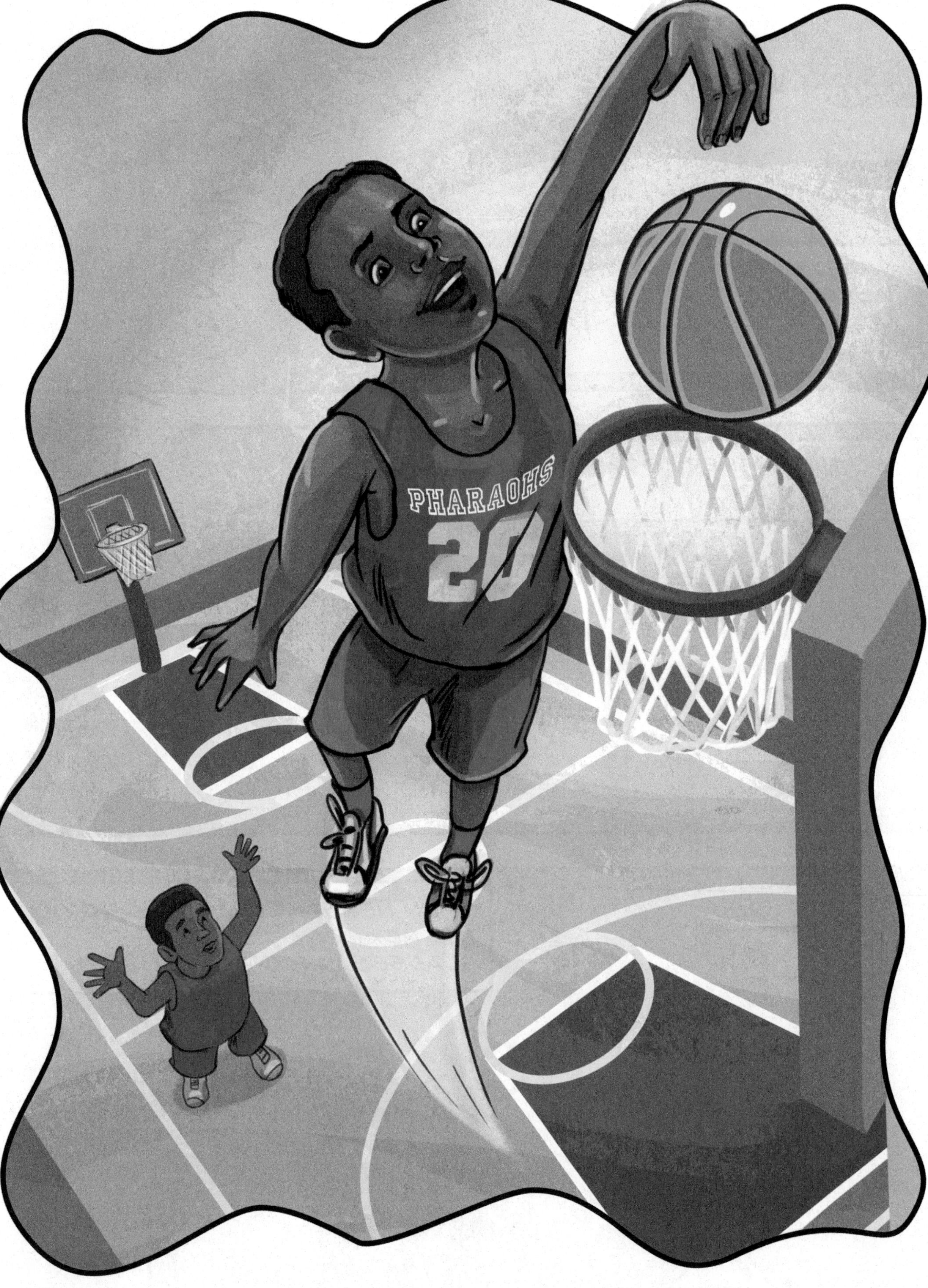
PHARAOHS
20

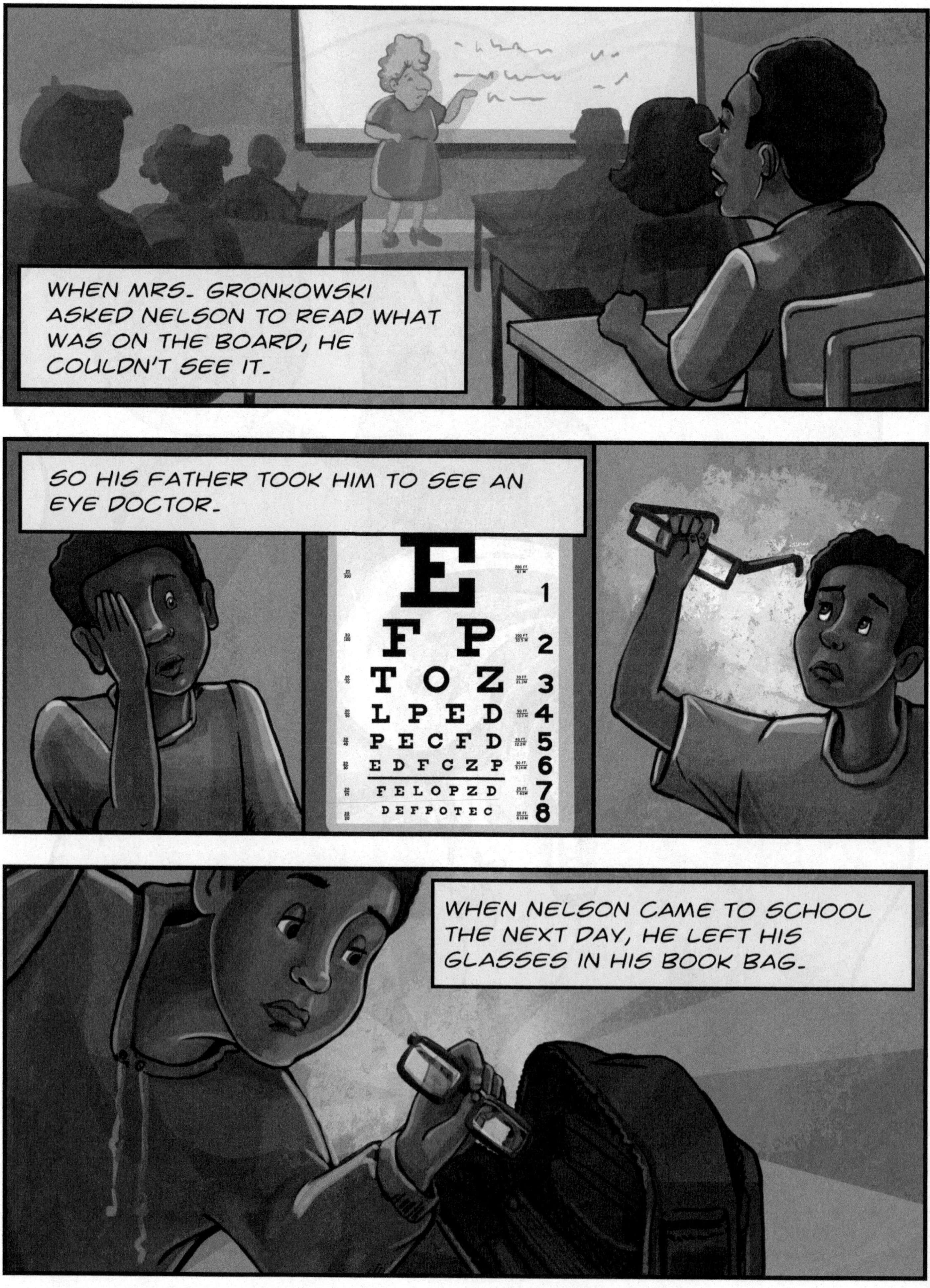
WHEN MRS. GRONKOWSKI ASKED NELSON TO READ WHAT WAS ON THE BOARD, HE COULDN'T SEE IT.
SO HIS FATHER TOOK HIM TO SEE AN EYE DOCTOR.
E 1
F P 2
T O Z 3
L P E D 4
P E C F D 5
E D F C Z P 6
F E L O P Z D 7
D E F P O T E C 8
WHEN NELSON CAME TO SCHOOL THE NEXT DAY, HE LEFT HIS GLASSES IN HIS BOOK BAG.

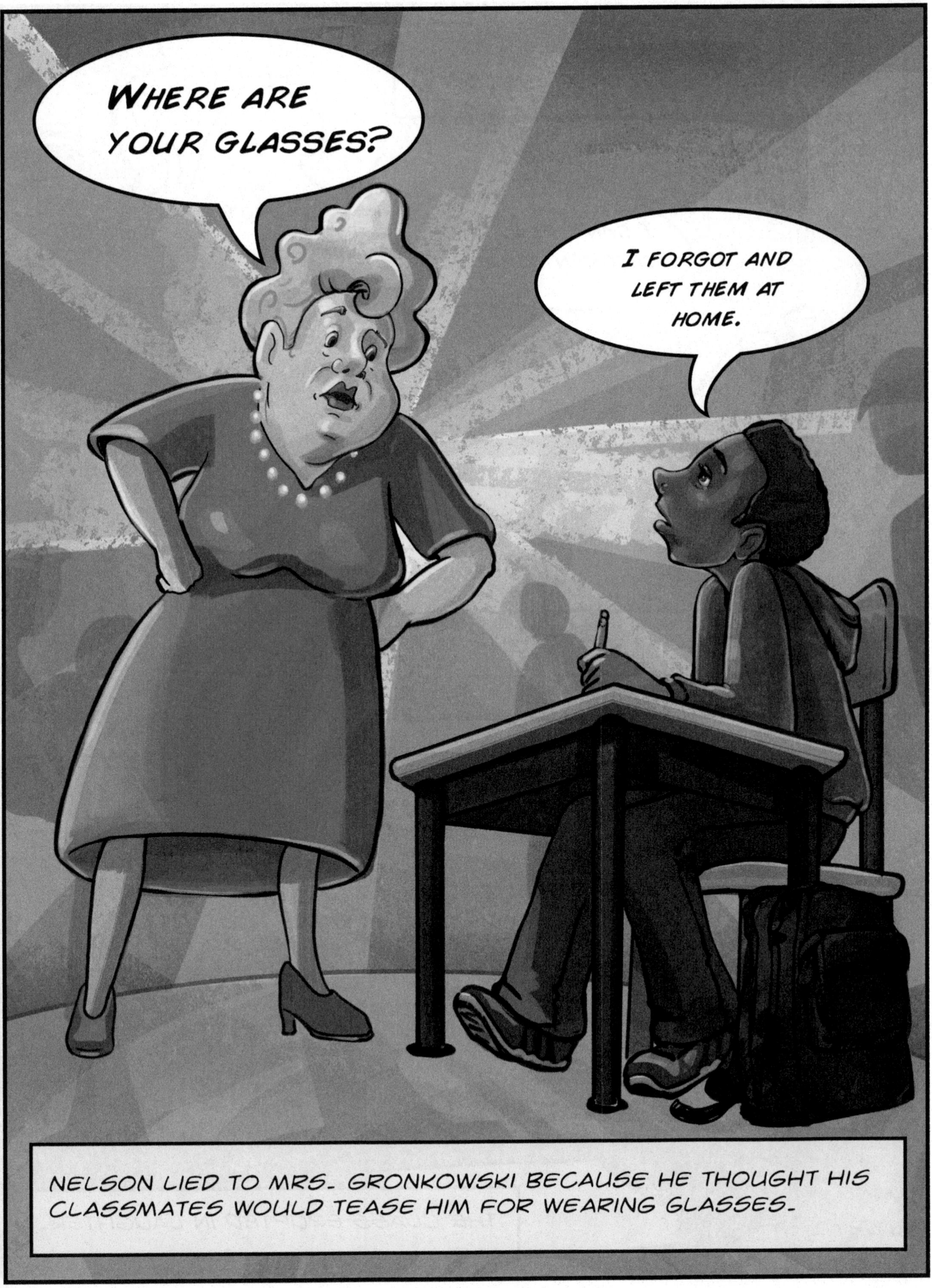
WHERE ARE YOUR GLASSES?
I FORGOT AND LEFT THEM AT HOME.
NELSON LIED TO MRS. GRONKOWSKI BECAUSE HE THOUGHT HIS CLASSMATES WOULD TEASE HIM FOR WEARING GLASSES.

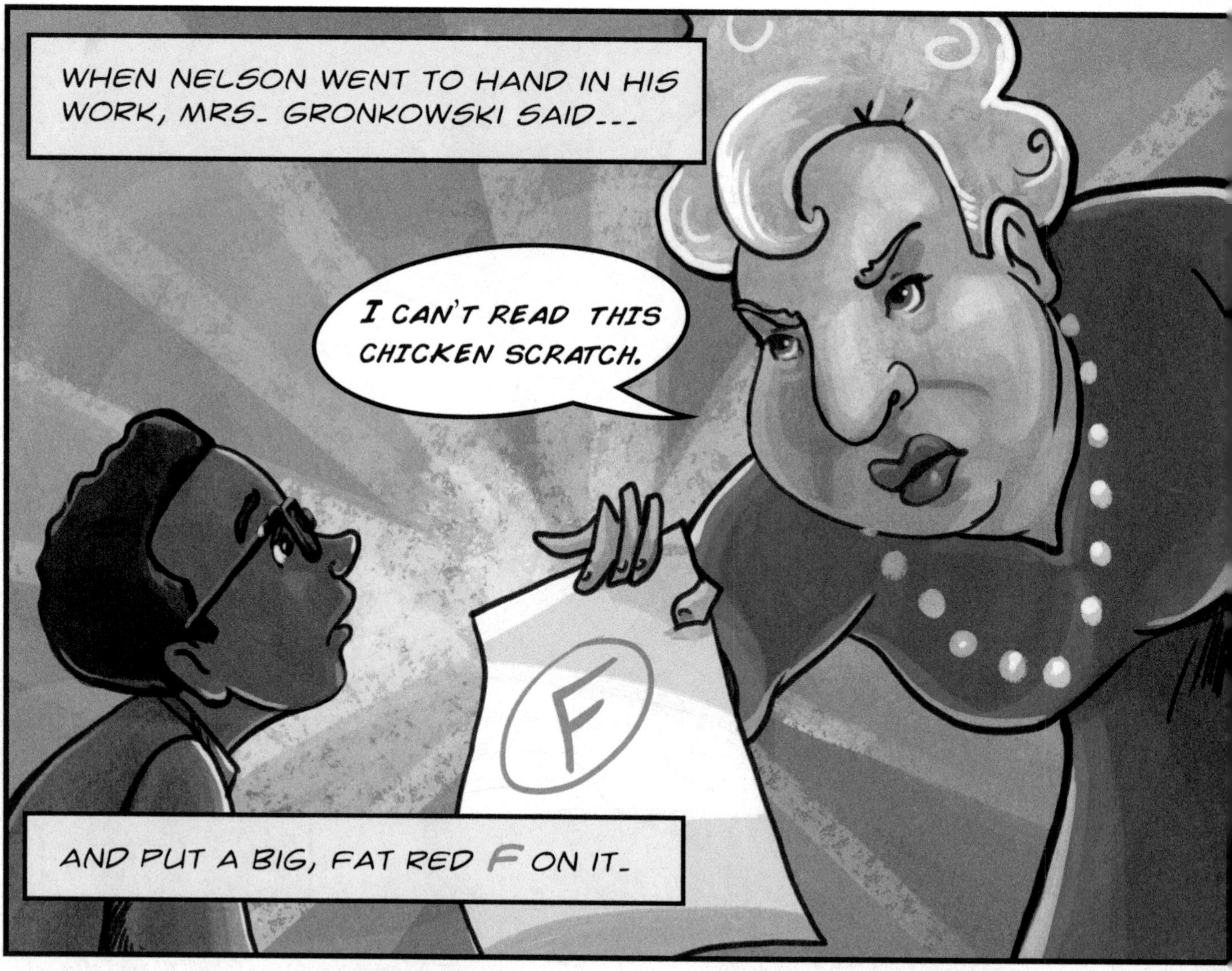
WHEN NELSON WENT TO HAND IN HIS WORK, MRS. GRONKOWSKI SAID...
I CAN'T READ THIS CHICKEN SCRATCH.
AND PUT A BIG, FAT RED F ON IT.

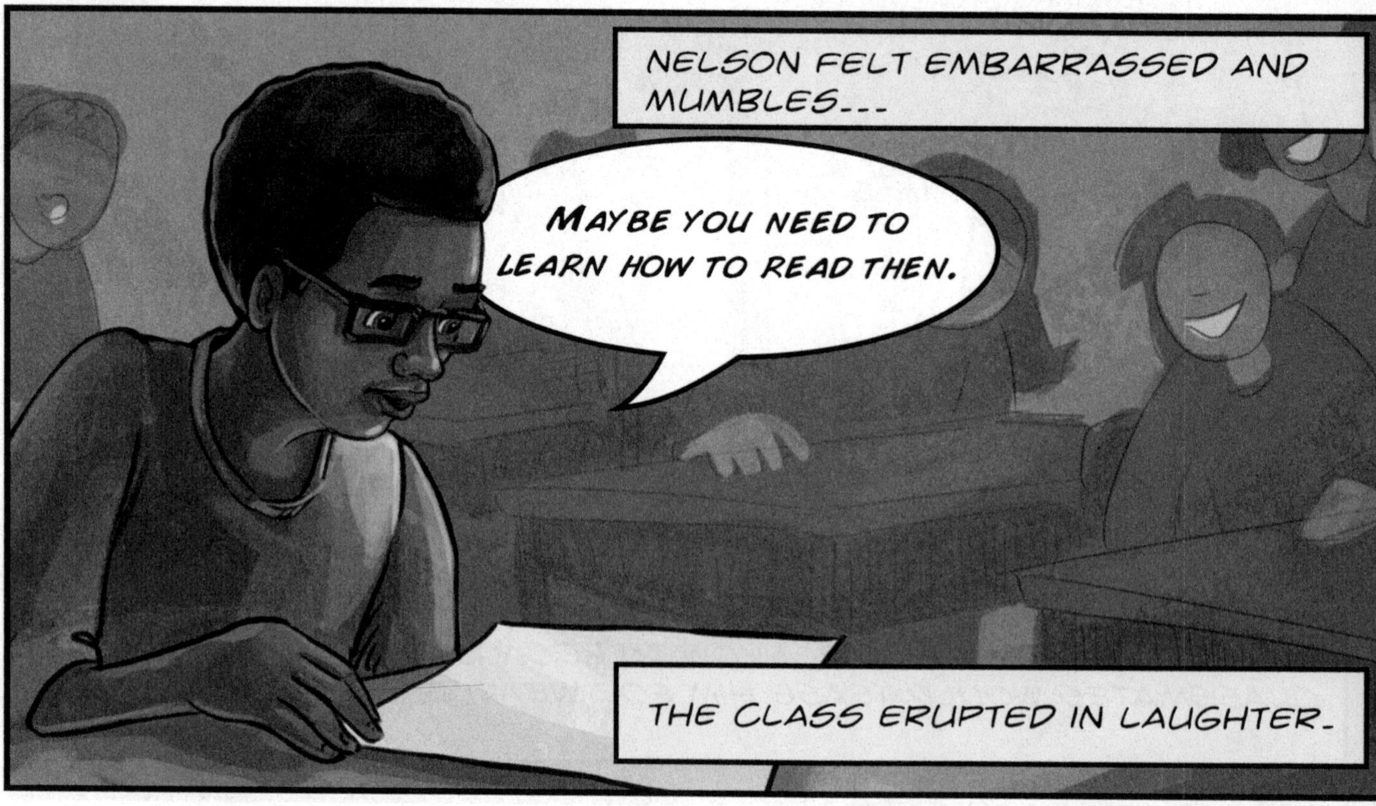
NELSON FELT EMBARRASSED AND MUMBLES...
MAYBE YOU NEED TO LEARN HOW TO READ THEN.
THE CLASS ERUPTED IN LAUGHTER.

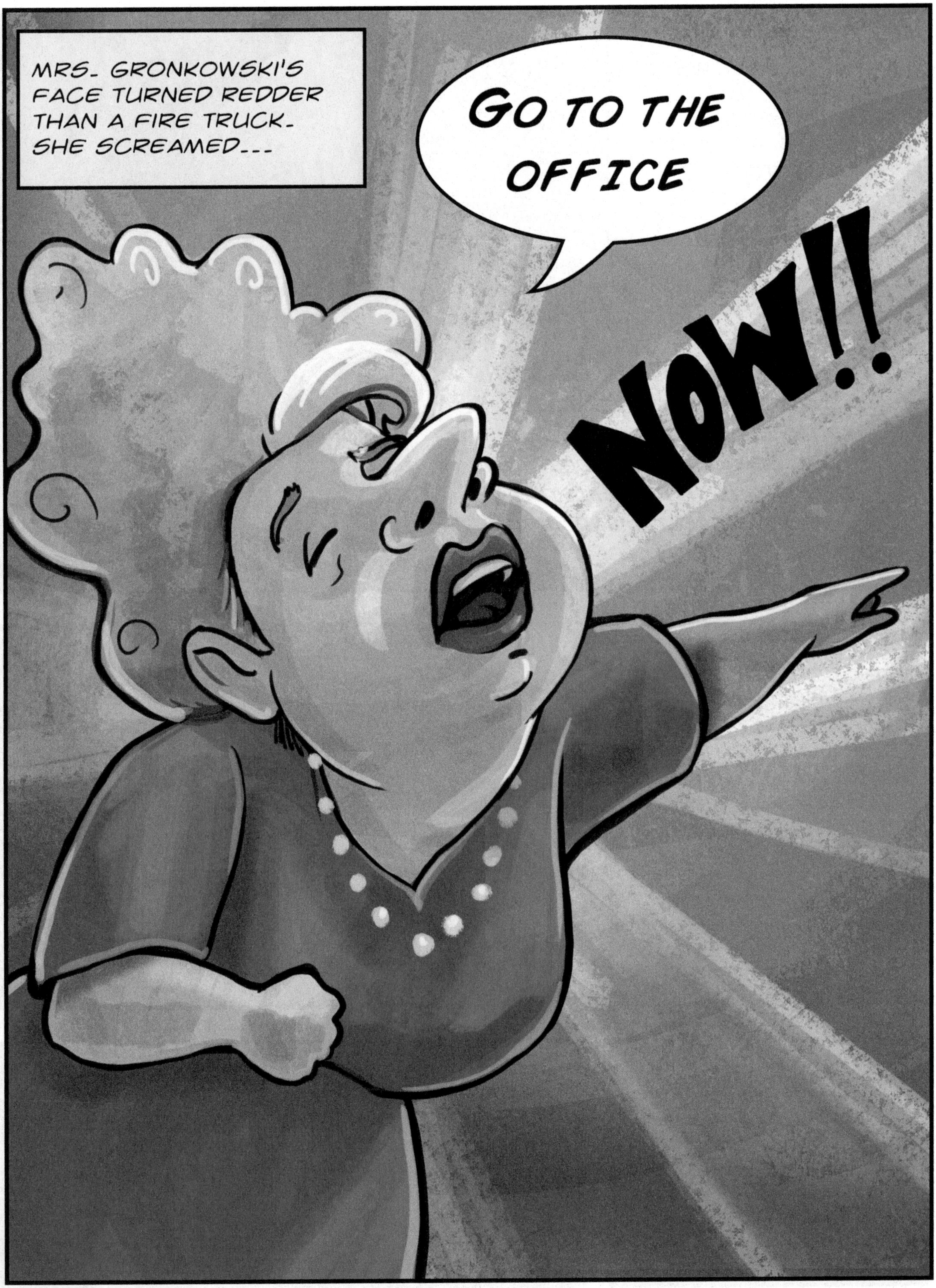
MRS. GRONKOWSKI'S FACE TURNED REDDER THAN A FIRE TRUCK. SHE SCREAMED...
GO TO THE OFFICE
NOW!!

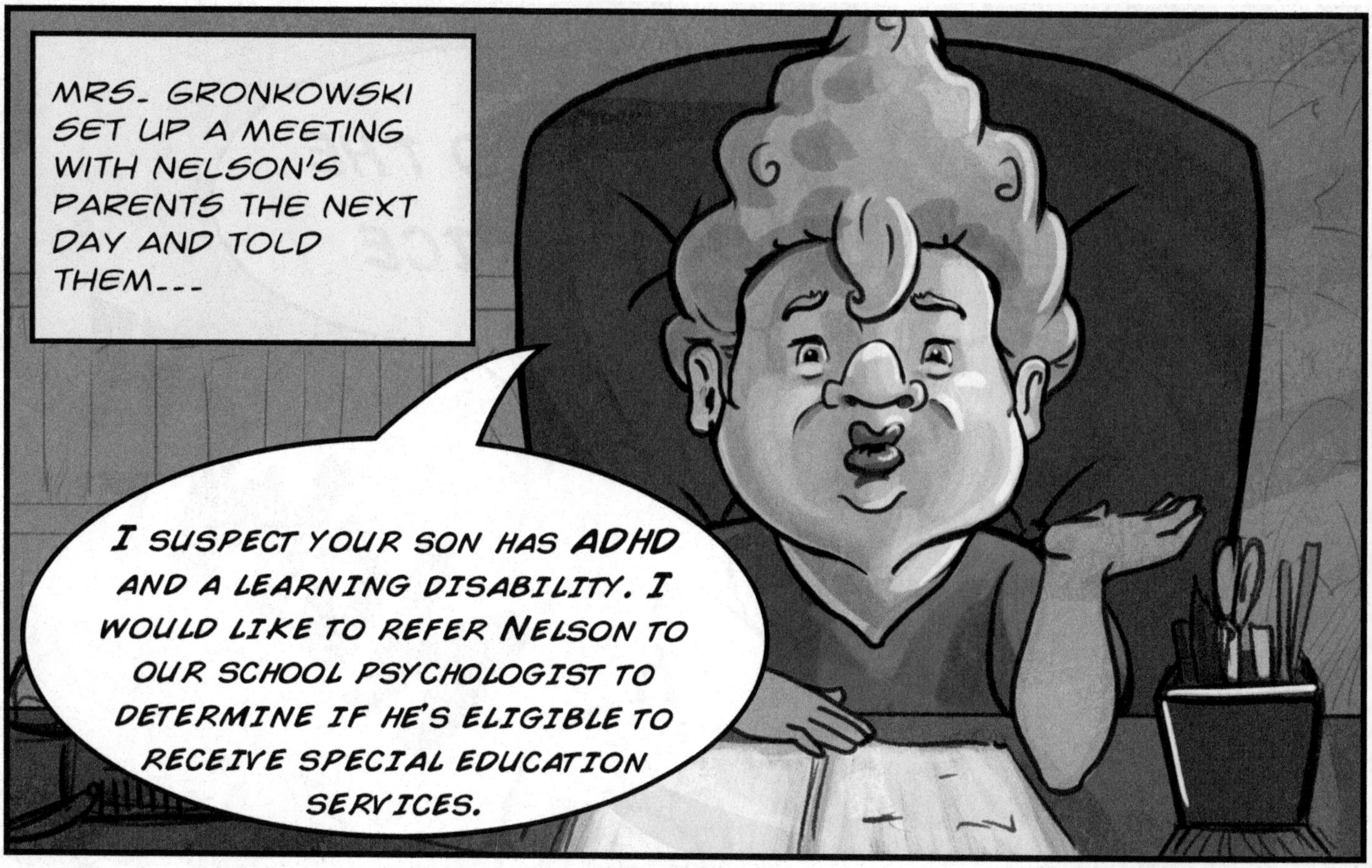
MRS. GRONKOWSKI SET UP A MEETING WITH NELSON'S PARENTS THE NEXT DAY AND TOLD THEM...
I SUSPECT YOUR SON HAS ADHD AND A LEARNING DISABILITY. I WOULD LIKE TO REFER NELSON TO OUR SCHOOL PSYCHOLOGIST TO DETERMINE IF HE'S ELIGIBLE TO RECEIVE SPECIAL EDUCATION SERVICES.

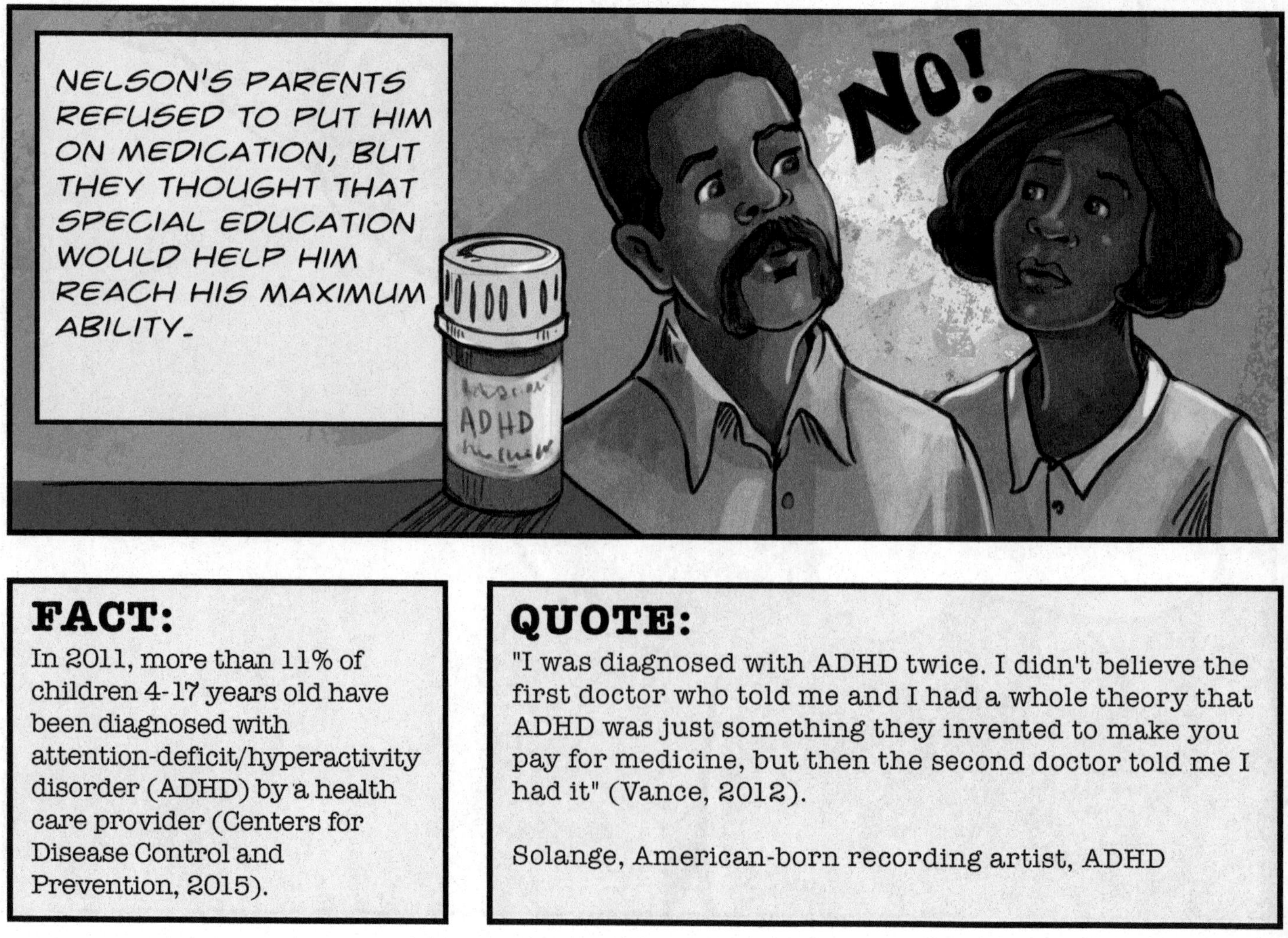
NELSON'S PARENTS REFUSED TO PUT HIM ON MEDICATION, BUT THEY THOUGHT THAT SPECIAL EDUCATION WOULD HELP HIM REACH HIS MAXIMUM ABILITY.
NO!
ADHD

FACT:

In 2011, more than 11% of children 4-17 years old have been diagnosed with attention-deficit/hyperactivity disorder (ADHD) by a health care provider (Centers for Disease Control and Prevention, 2015).

QUOTE:

"I was diagnosed with ADHD twice. I didn't believe the first doctor who told me and I had a whole theory that ADHD was just something they invented to make you pay for medicine, but then the second doctor told me I had it" (Vance, 2012).

Solange, American-born recording artist, ADHD

THERE'S NOTHING WRONG WITH YOU BABY. YOU JUST NEED SOME EXTRA HELP.
IT'S NOT FAIR. I WON'T BE IN CLASS WITH MY FRIENDS AND EVERYONE WILL THINK I'M SLOW.
YOU'RE NOT SLOW; I'VE ALWAYS TOLD YOU THAT YOU WERE SMART.
YOUR DAD AND I JUST WANT THE BEST FOR YOU AND THE SCHOOL THINKS THIS PROGRAM WILL HELP.

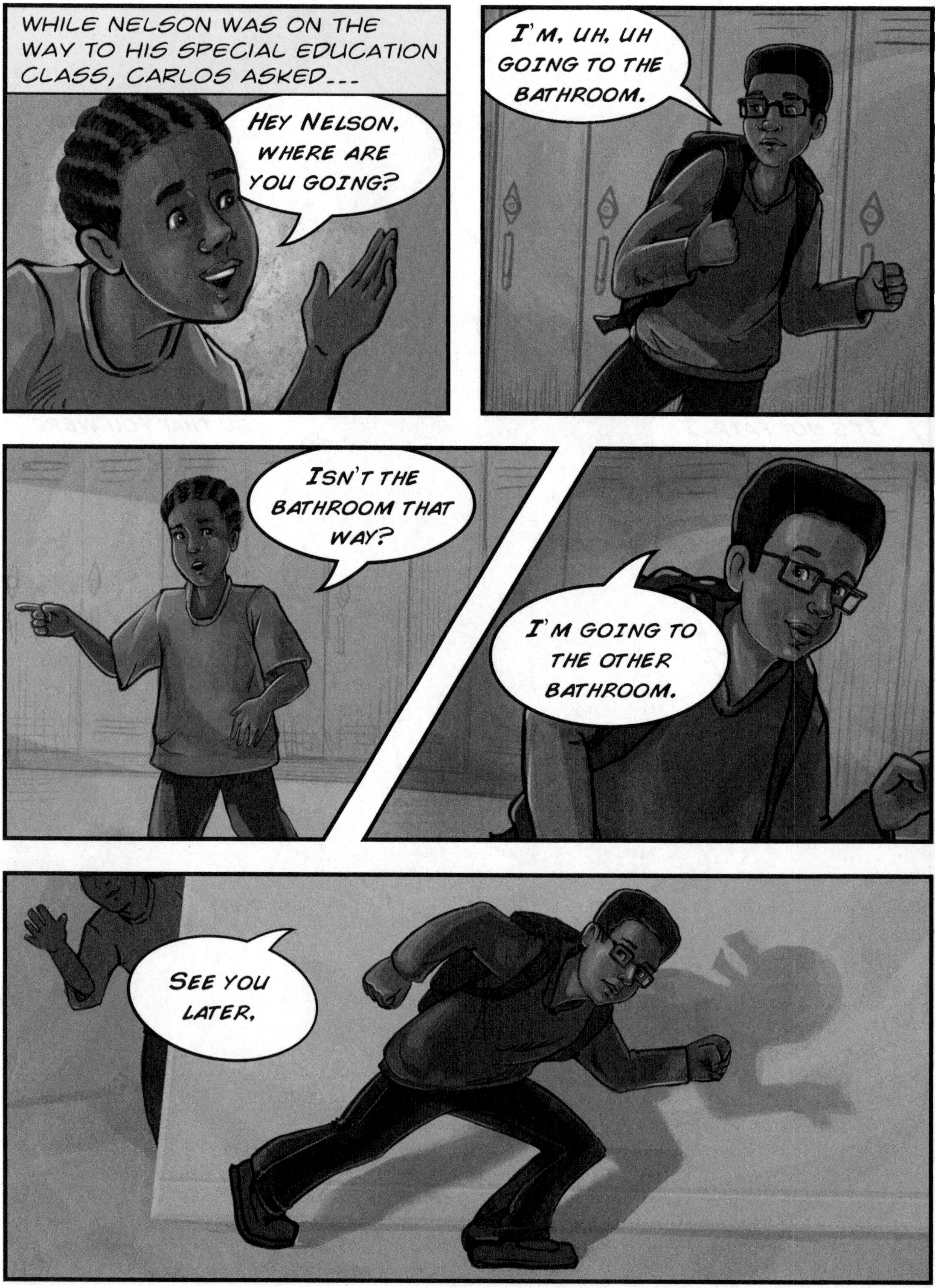
WHILE NELSON WAS ON THE WAY TO HIS SPECIAL EDUCATION CLASS, CARLOS ASKED...
HEY NELSON, WHERE ARE YOU GOING?
I'M, UH, UH GOING TO THE BATHROOM.
ISN'T THE BATHROOM THAT WAY?
I'M GOING TO THE OTHER BATHROOM.
SEE YOU LATER.

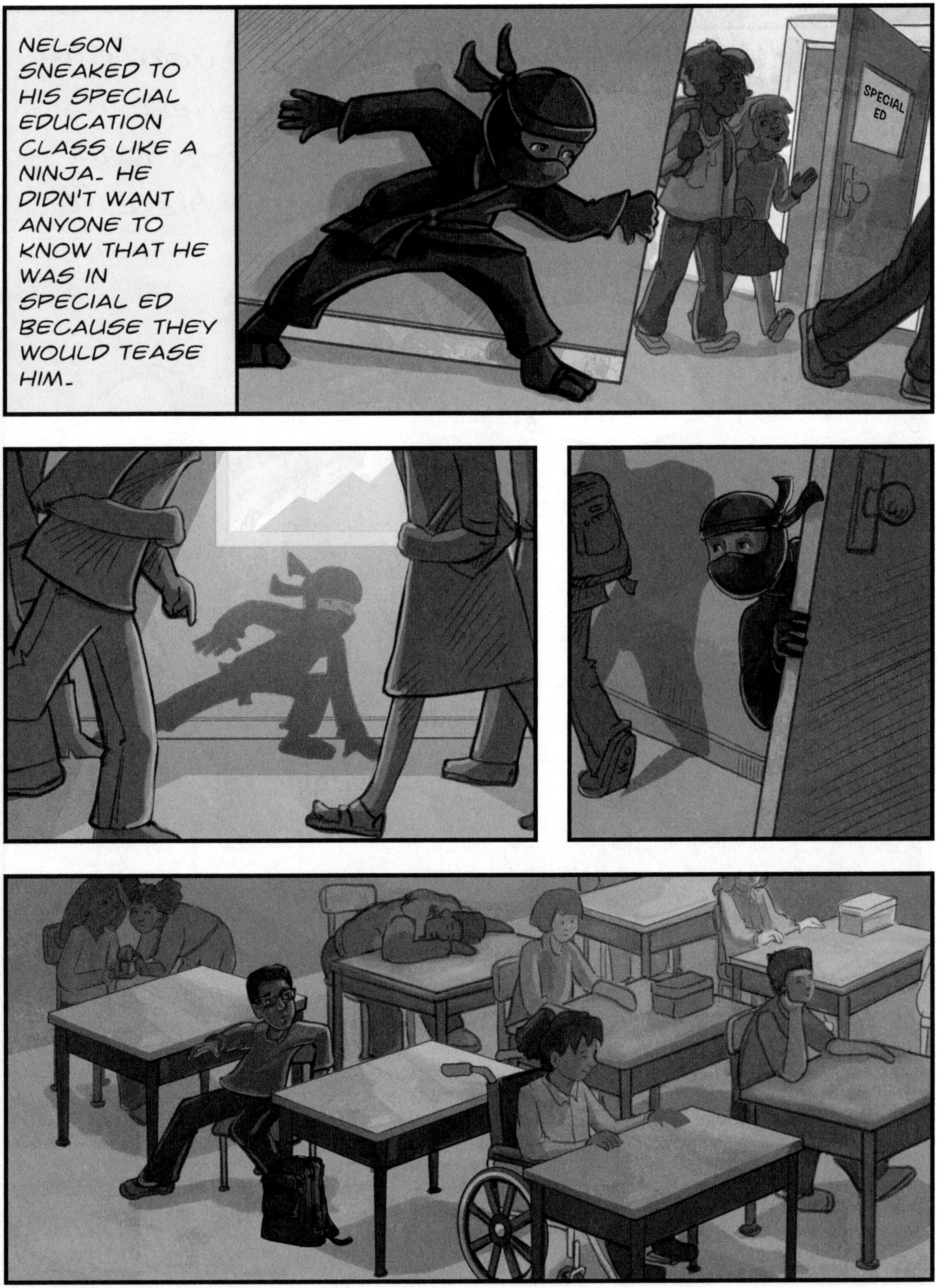
NELSON SNEAKED TO HIS SPECIAL EDUCATION CLASS LIKE A NINJA. HE DIDN'T WANT ANYONE TO KNOW THAT HE WAS IN SPECIAL ED BECAUSE THEY WOULD TEASE HIM.
SPECIAL ED

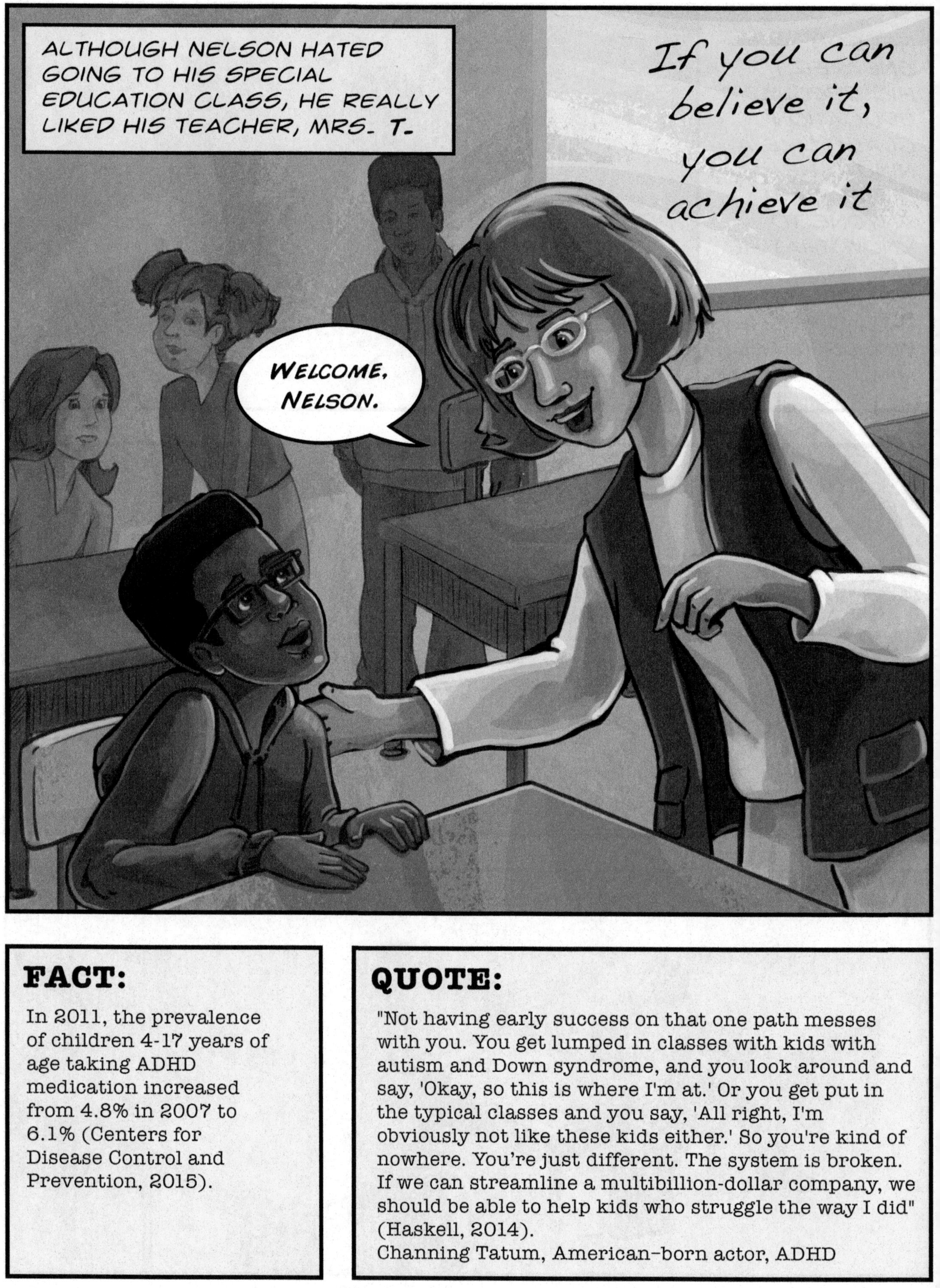
ALTHOUGH NELSON HATED GOING TO HIS SPECIAL EDUCATION CLASS, HE REALLY LIKED HIS TEACHER, MRS. T.
If you can believe it, you can achieve it
WELCOME, NELSON.

FACT:

In 2011, the prevalence of children 4-17 years of age taking ADHD medication increased from 4.8% in 2007 to 6.1% (Centers for Disease Control and Prevention, 2015).

QUOTE:

"Not having early success on that one path messes with you. You get lumped in classes with kids with autism and Down syndrome, and you look around and say, 'Okay, so this is where I'm at.' Or you get put in the typical classes and you say, 'All right, I'm obviously not like these kids either.' So you're kind of nowhere. You're just different. The system is broken. If we can streamline a multibillion-dollar company, we should be able to help kids who struggle the way I did" (Haskell, 2014).
Channing Tatum, American-born actor, ADHD

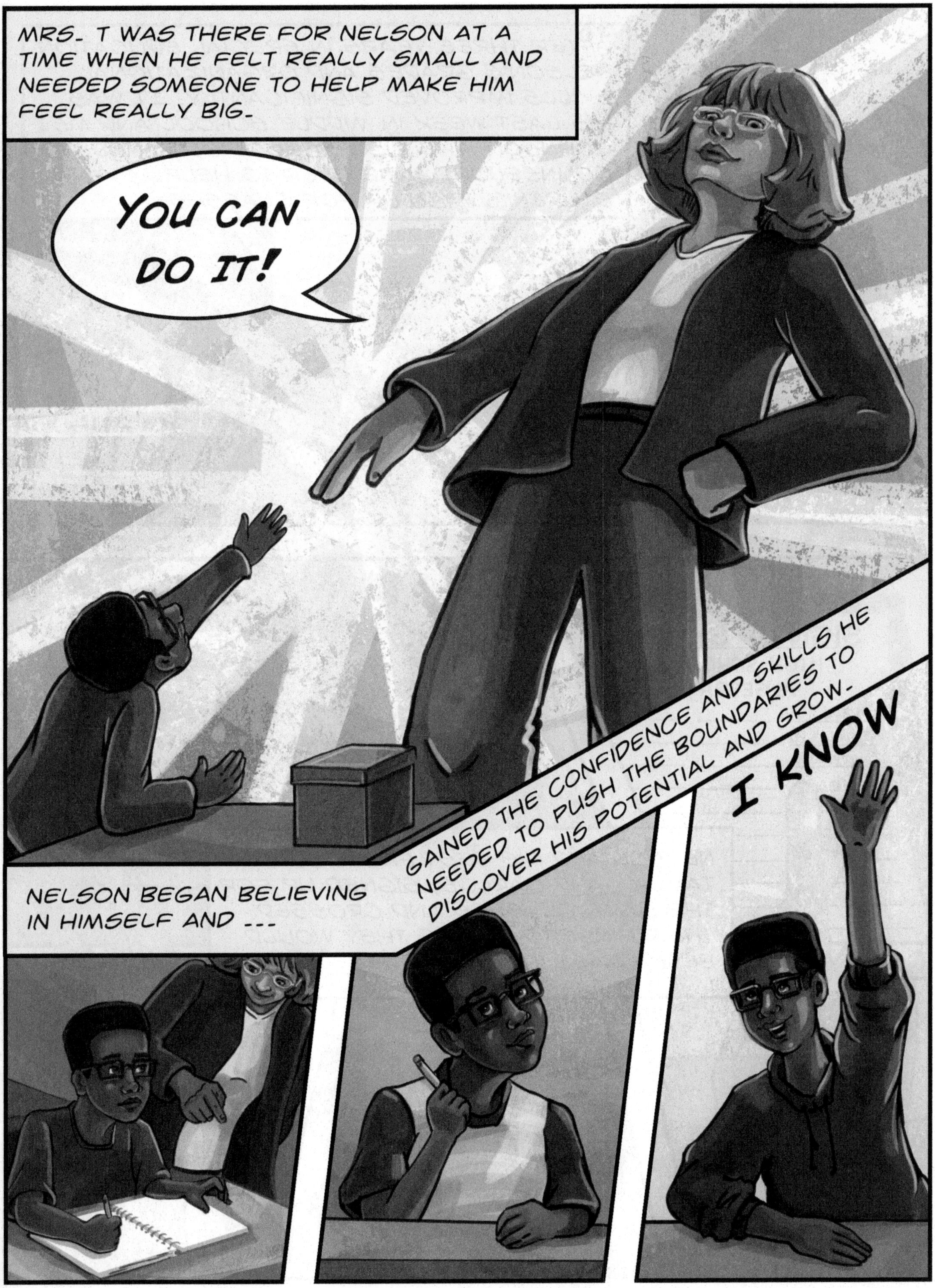
MRS. T WAS THERE FOR NELSON AT A TIME WHEN HE FELT REALLY SMALL AND NEEDED SOMEONE TO HELP MAKE HIM FEEL REALLY BIG.
YOU CAN DO IT!
NELSON BEGAN BELIEVING IN HIMSELF AND ...
GAINED THE CONFIDENCE AND SKILLS HE NEEDED TO PUSH THE BOUNDARIES TO DISCOVER HIS POTENTIAL AND GROW.
I KNOW

AFTER THREE YEARS IN SPECIAL EDUCATION, NELSON'S GRADES AND ORGANIZATIONAL SKILLS IMPROVED SIGNIFICANTLY. IT WAS HIS LAST WEEK IN MIDDLE SCHOOL AND MS. JOHNSON, THE HIGH SCHOOL GUIDANCE COUNSELOR, CAME OVER TO HELP STUDENTS SIGN UP FOR CLASSES.

SIGN UP SHEET
HIGH SCHOOL
ALGEBRA

Jack Kelter
Adnan
Tameka
Carlos
Nelson

NELSON AND HIS BEST FRIENDS, TAMEKA AND CARLOS, SIGNED UP FOR THE SAME CLASSES AND CROSSED THEIR FINGERS HOPING THEY WOULD BE IN CLASS TOGETHER NEXT YEAR.

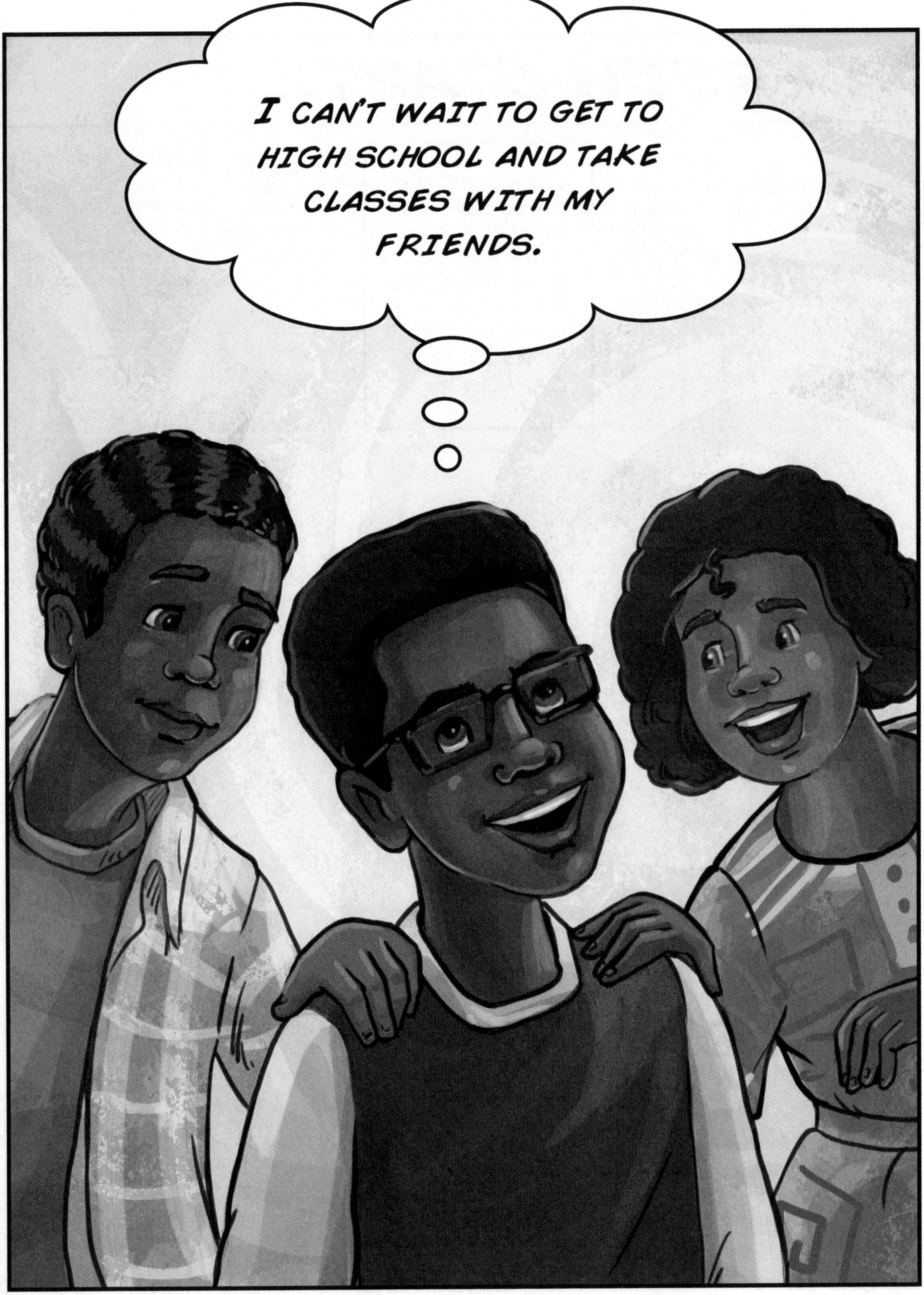
I CAN'T WAIT TO GET TO HIGH SCHOOL AND TAKE CLASSES WITH MY FRIENDS.

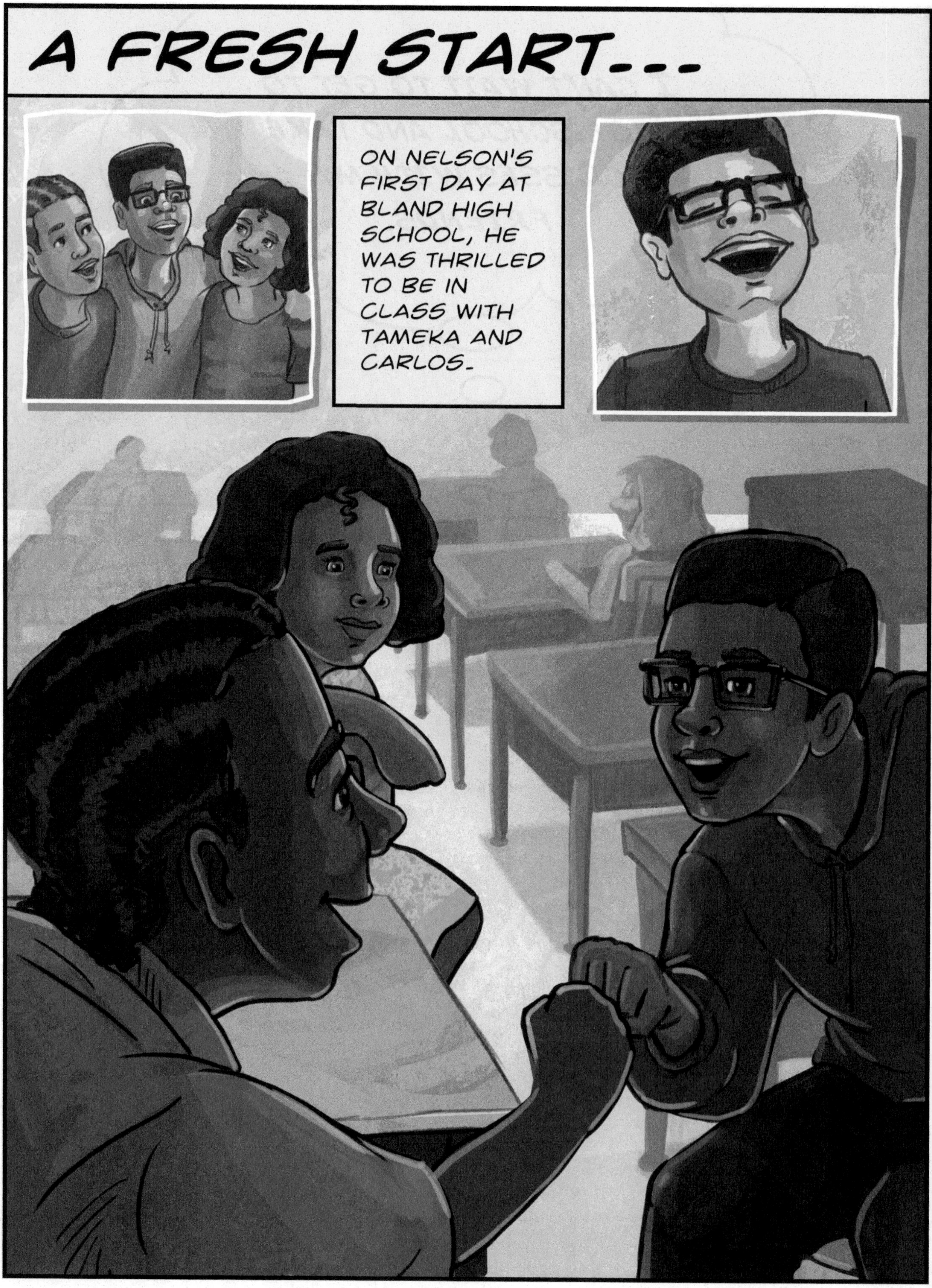
A FRESH START...
ON NELSON'S FIRST DAY AT BLAND HIGH SCHOOL, HE WAS THRILLED TO BE IN CLASS WITH TAMEKA AND CARLOS.

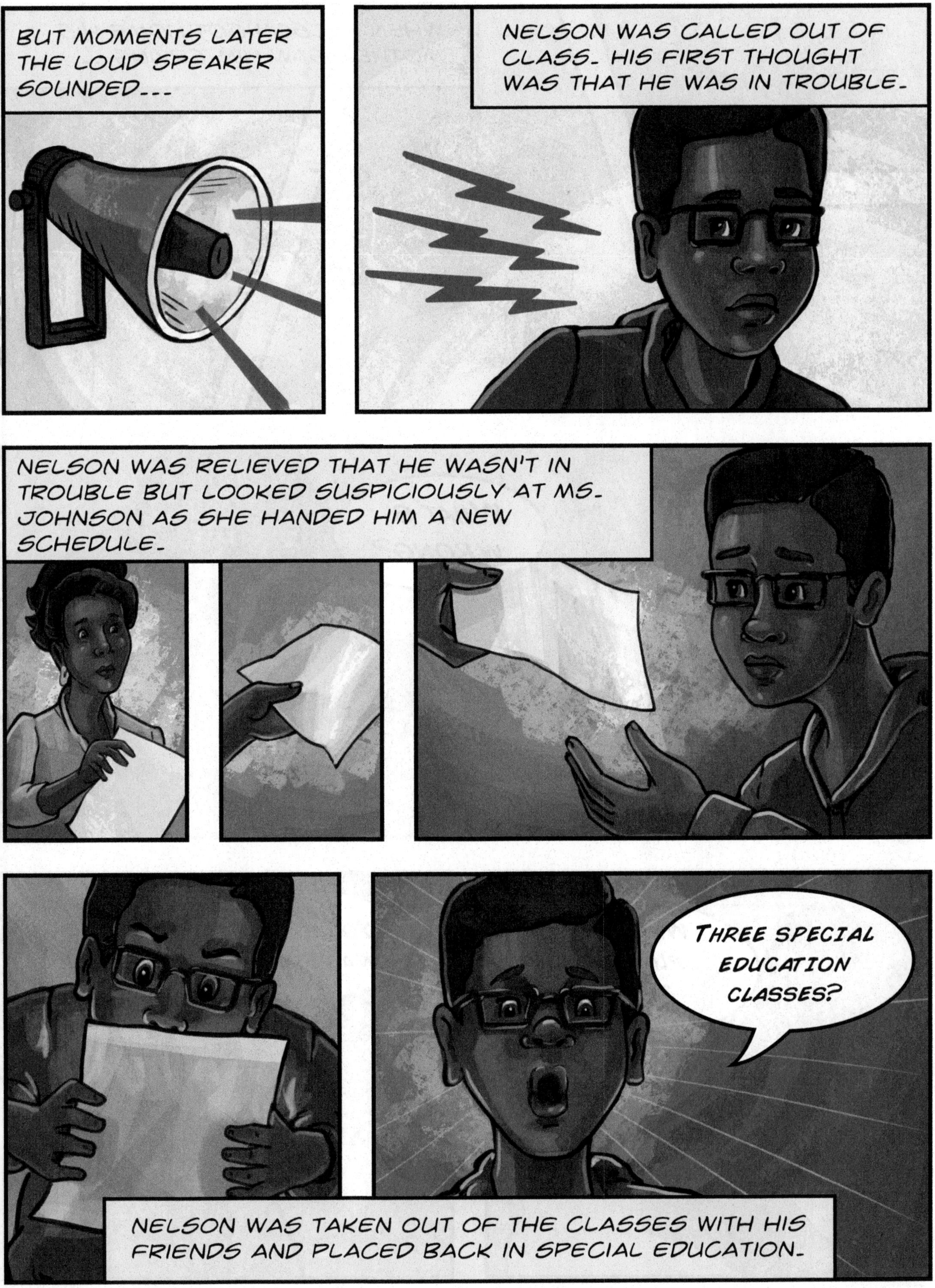
BUT MOMENTS LATER THE LOUD SPEAKER SOUNDED...
NELSON WAS CALLED OUT OF CLASS. HIS FIRST THOUGHT WAS THAT HE WAS IN TROUBLE.
NELSON WAS RELIEVED THAT HE WASN'T IN TROUBLE BUT LOOKED SUSPICIOUSLY AT MS. JOHNSON AS SHE HANDED HIM A NEW SCHEDULE.
THREE SPECIAL EDUCATION CLASSES?
NELSON WAS TAKEN OUT OF THE CLASSES WITH HIS FRIENDS AND PLACED BACK IN SPECIAL EDUCATION.

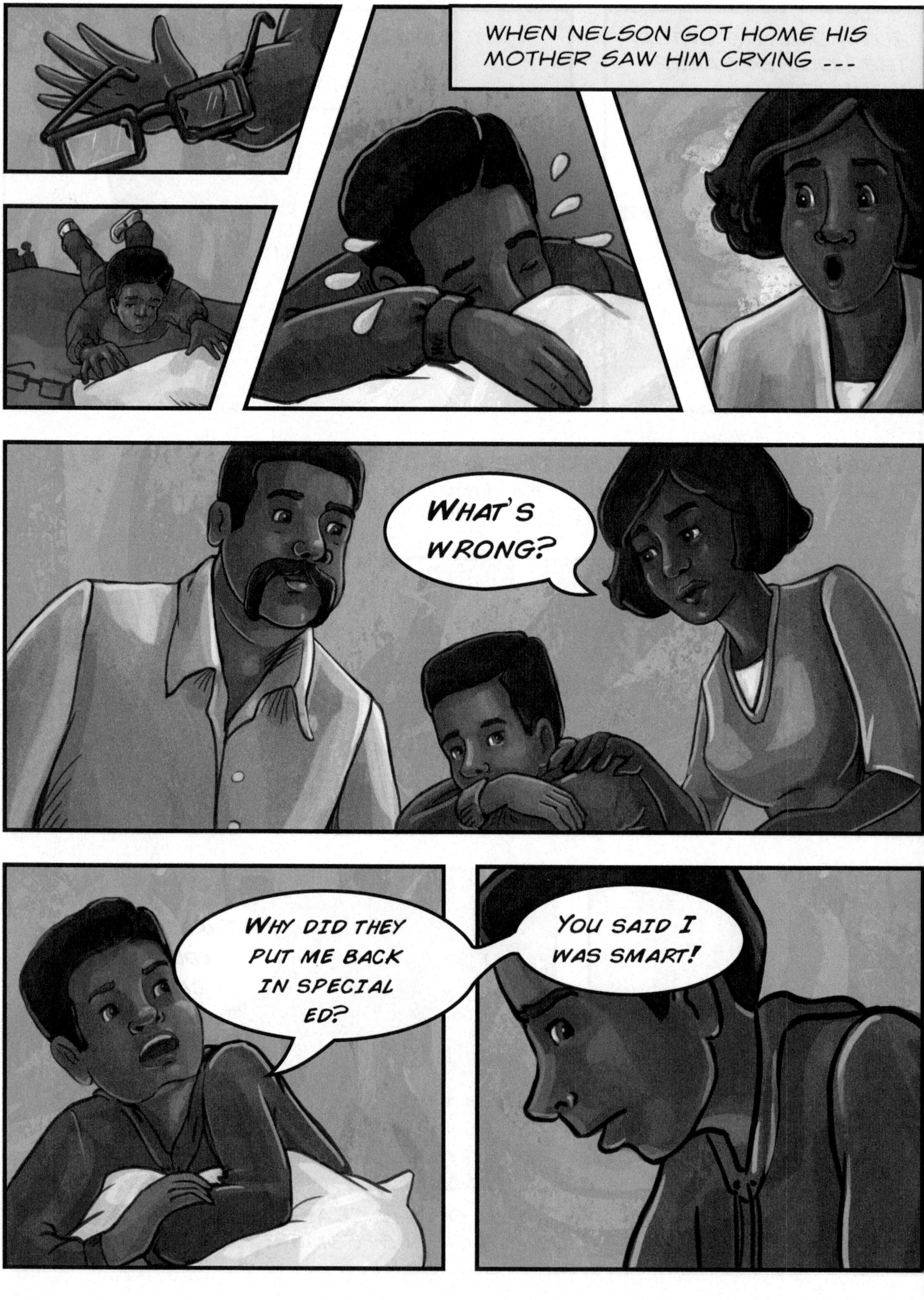
WHEN NELSON GOT HOME HIS MOTHER SAW HIM CRYING ---
WHAT'S WRONG?
WHY DID THEY PUT ME BACK IN SPECIAL ED?
YOU SAID I WAS SMART!

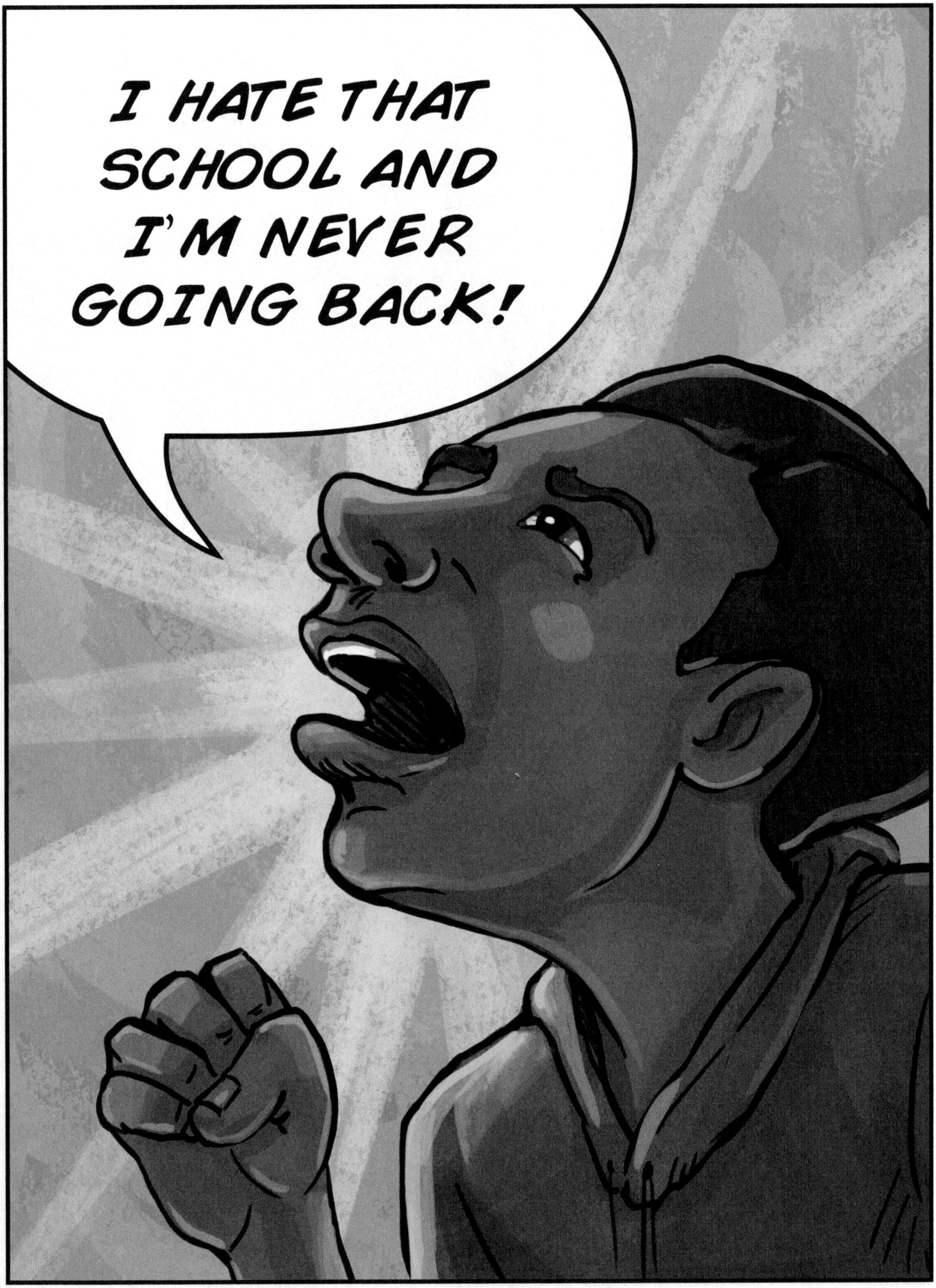
I HATE THAT SCHOOL AND I'M NEVER GOING BACK!

THE NEXT DAY NELSON'S PARENTS MET WITH MS. JOHNSON AND SAID...
MY SON CAME HOME CRYING YESTERDAY AND SAID YOU PUT HIM BACK IN SPECIAL EDUCATION.
WE WANT OUR SON OUT OF THOSE CLASSES NOW!
IN
OUT

I'M SO SORRY, THERE MUST'VE BEEN SOME MISTAKE. I WILL TAKE YOUR SON OUT OF THOSE CLASSES IMMEDIATELY.
BUT HE WILL NEED TO BE PLACED IN DEVELOPMENTAL ALGEBRA.
RECEPTION

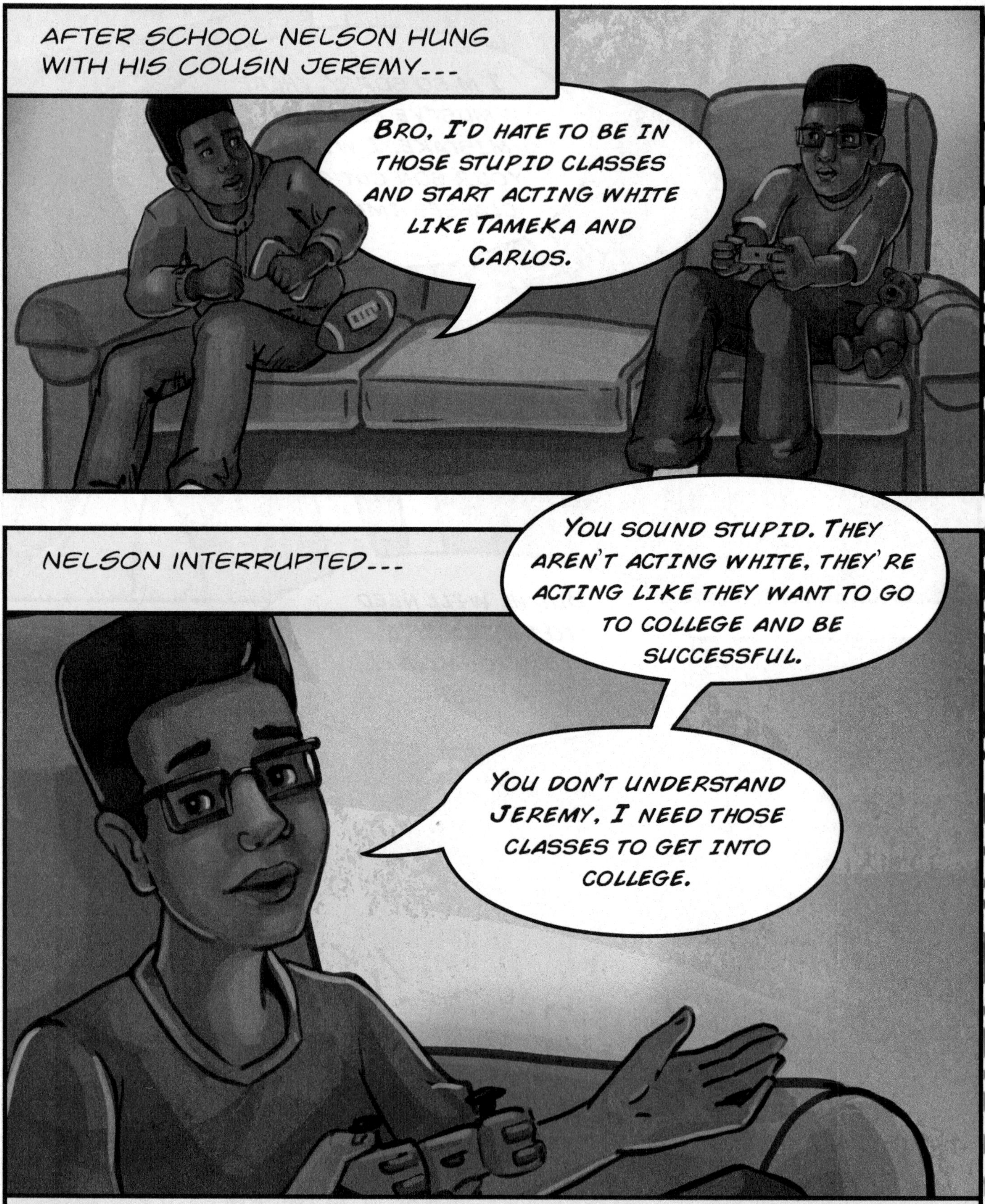
AFTER SCHOOL NELSON HUNG WITH HIS COUSIN JEREMY...
BRO, I'D HATE TO BE IN THOSE STUPID CLASSES AND START ACTING WHITE LIKE TAMEKA AND CARLOS.
NELSON INTERRUPTED...
YOU SOUND STUPID. THEY AREN'T ACTING WHITE, THEY'RE ACTING LIKE THEY WANT TO GO TO COLLEGE AND BE SUCCESSFUL.
YOU DON'T UNDERSTAND JEREMY, I NEED THOSE CLASSES TO GET INTO COLLEGE.

NOTE:

"The fear of being accused of "acting white" causes a social and psychological situation which diminishes black students' academic effort and thus leads to underachievement" (Fordham and Ogbu, 1986, p. 176).

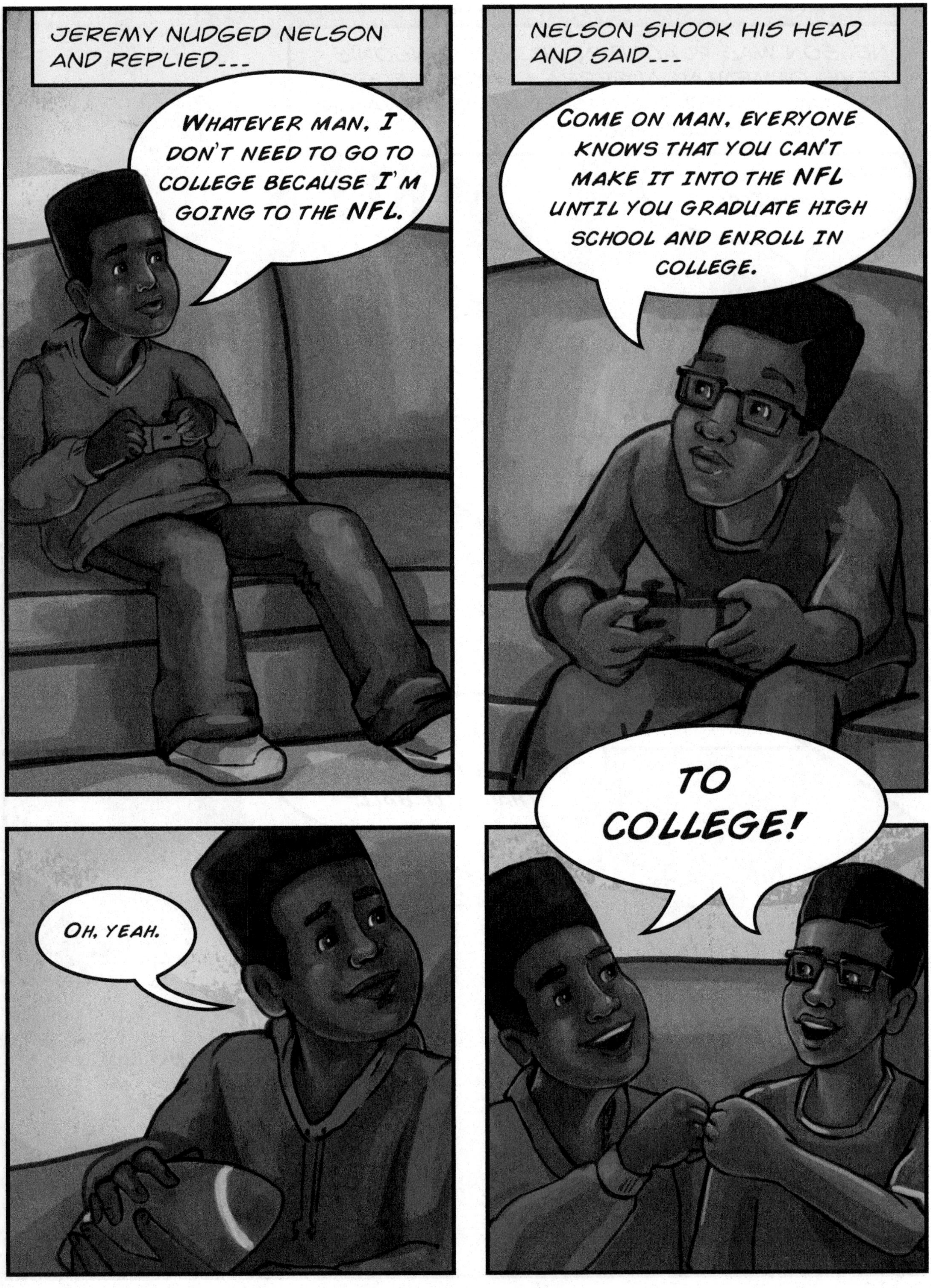
JEREMY NUDGED NELSON AND REPLIED...
WHATEVER MAN, I DON'T NEED TO GO TO COLLEGE BECAUSE I'M GOING TO THE NFL.
NELSON SHOOK HIS HEAD AND SAID...
COME ON MAN, EVERYONE KNOWS THAT YOU CAN'T MAKE IT INTO THE NFL UNTIL YOU GRADUATE HIGH SCHOOL AND ENROLL IN COLLEGE.
OH, YEAH.
TO COLLEGE!

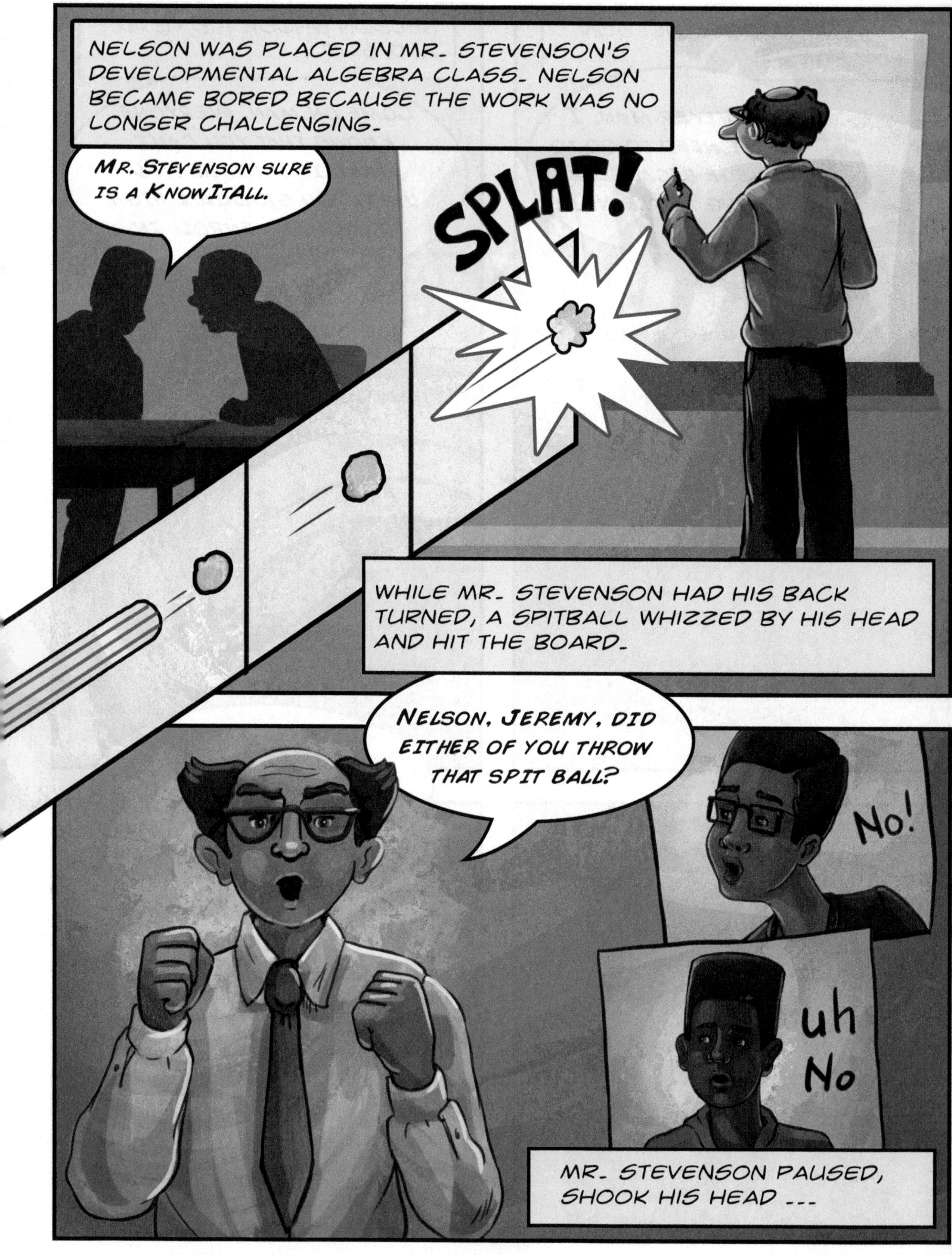
NELSON WAS PLACED IN MR. STEVENSON'S DEVELOPMENTAL ALGEBRA CLASS. NELSON BECAME BORED BECAUSE THE WORK WAS NO LONGER CHALLENGING.
MR. STEVENSON SURE IS A KNOWITALL.
SPLAT!
WHILE MR. STEVENSON HAD HIS BACK TURNED, A SPITBALL WHIZZED BY HIS HEAD AND HIT THE BOARD.
NELSON, JEREMY, DID EITHER OF YOU THROW THAT SPIT BALL?
No!
uh No
MR. STEVENSON PAUSED, SHOOK HIS HEAD ...

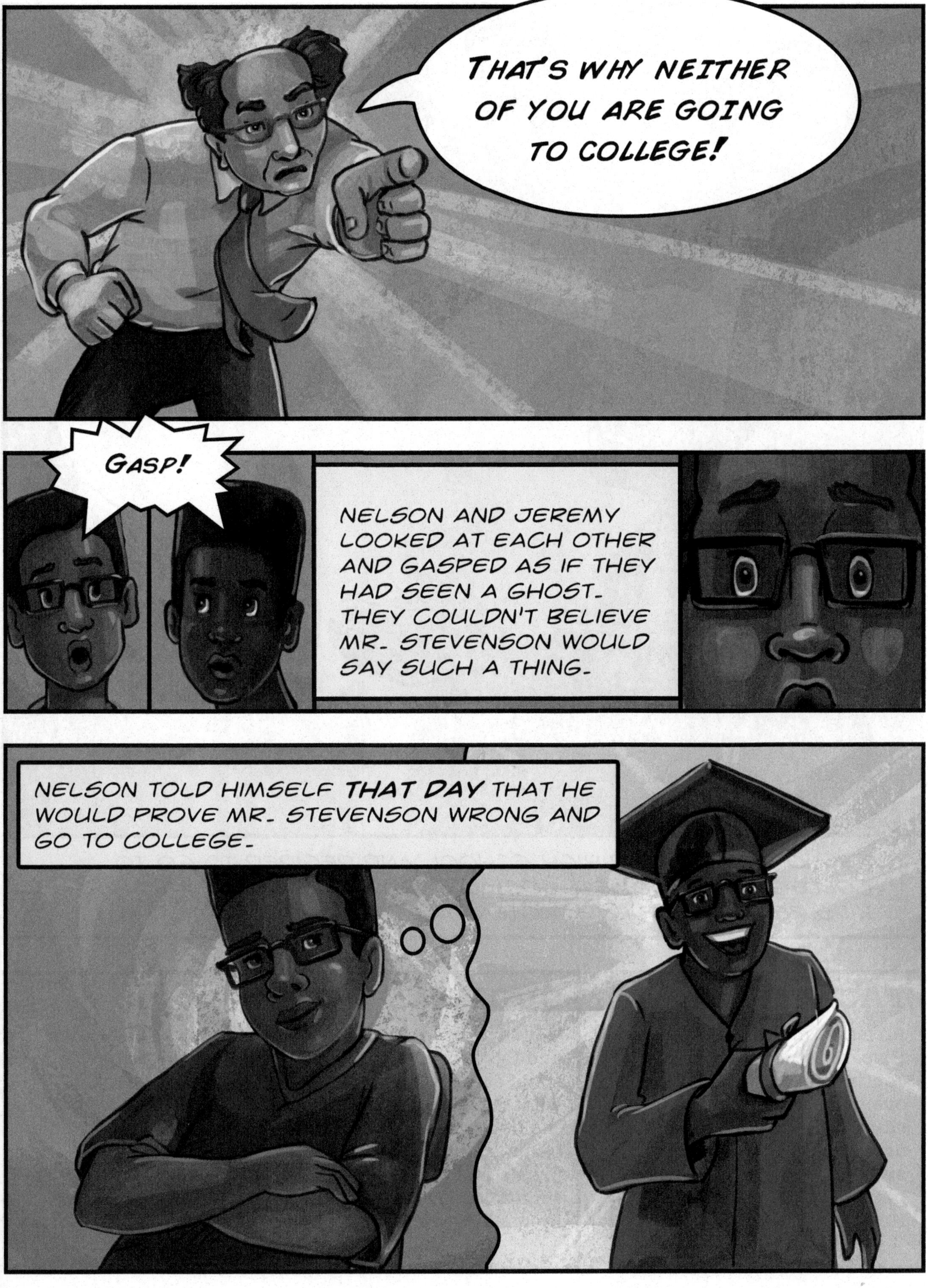
THAT'S WHY NEITHER OF YOU ARE GOING TO COLLEGE!
GASP!
NELSON AND JEREMY LOOKED AT EACH OTHER AND GASPED AS IF THEY HAD SEEN A GHOST. THEY COULDN'T BELIEVE MR. STEVENSON WOULD SAY SUCH A THING.
NELSON TOLD HIMSELF THAT DAY THAT HE WOULD PROVE MR. STEVENSON WRONG AND GO TO COLLEGE.

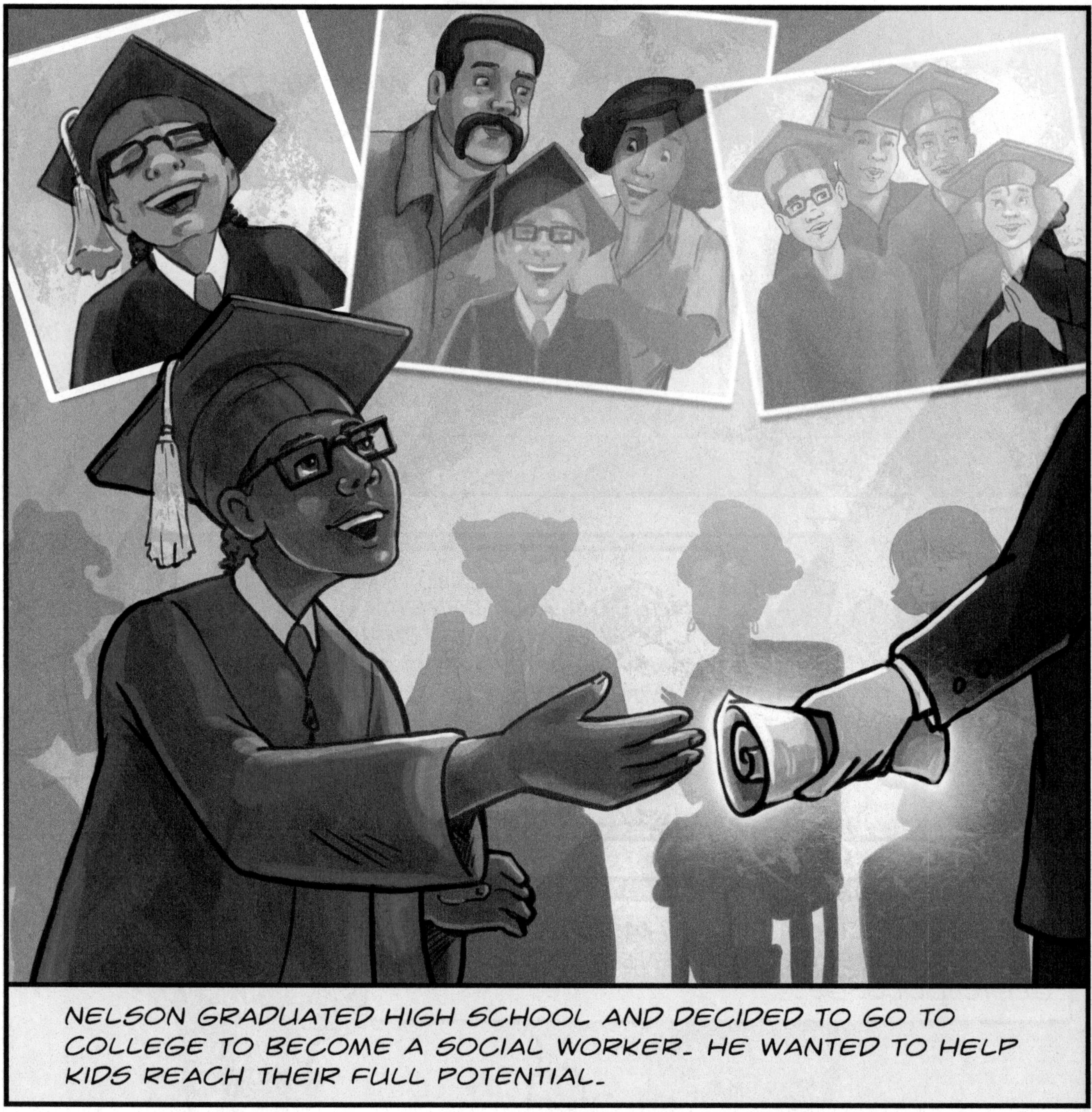
NELSON GRADUATED HIGH SCHOOL AND DECIDED TO GO TO COLLEGE TO BECOME A SOCIAL WORKER. HE WANTED TO HELP KIDS REACH THEIR FULL POTENTIAL.

FACT:

African-American and Hispanic students continue to be overrepresented in special education, have higher dropout rates, and are suspended and expelled at higher rates (Cortiella & Horowitz, 2014).

QUOTE:

"My teachers thought I was lazy and not very clever, and I got bored easily...thinking of all the things I could do once I left school. I couldn't always follow what was going on. On one of my last days at school, the headmaster said I would either end up in prison or become a millionaire. That was quite a startling prediction, but in some respects he was right on both counts" (Schwartz, 2012)!
Richard Branson, British-born business man, Dyslexia

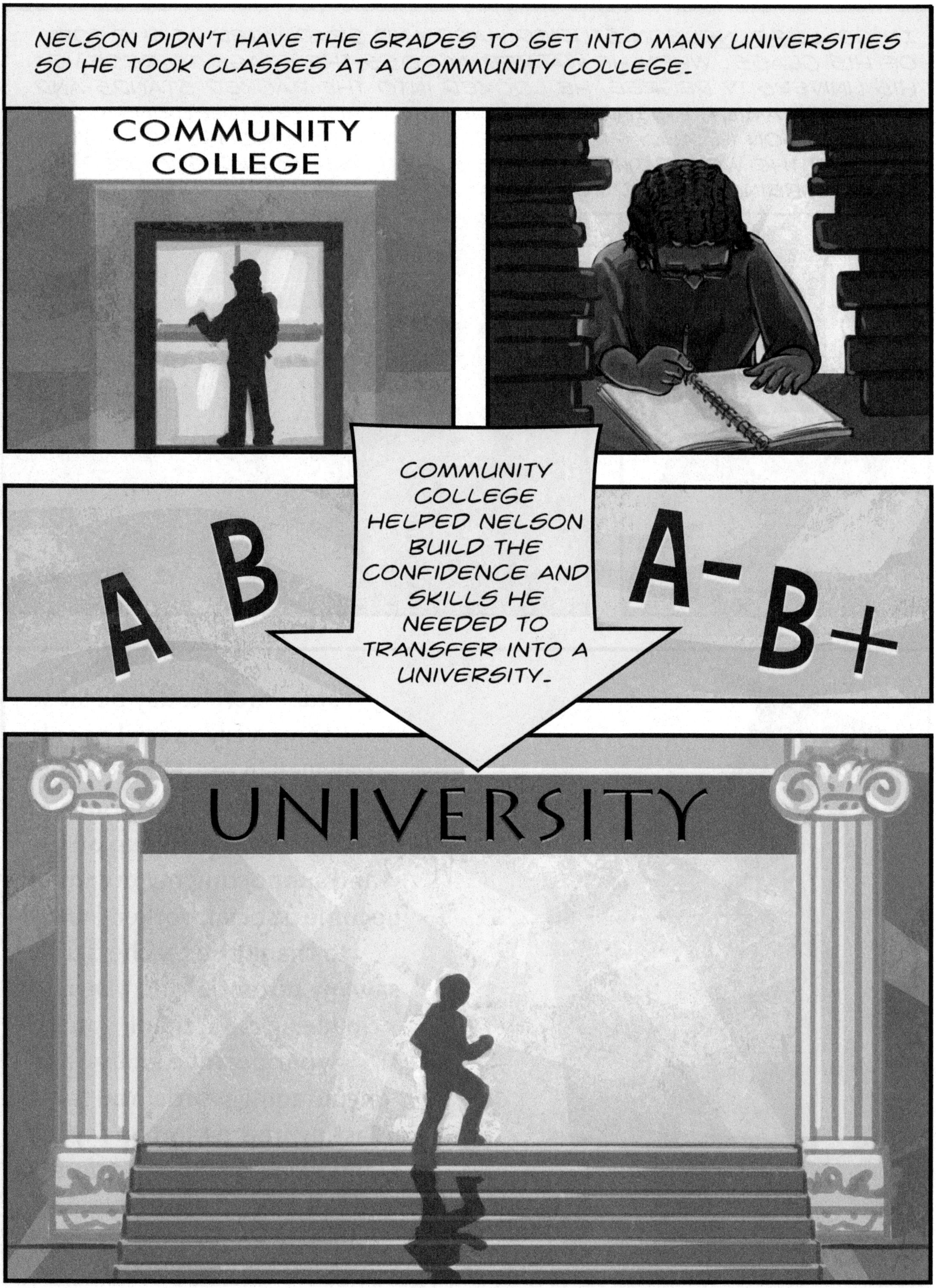
NELSON DIDN'T HAVE THE GRADES TO GET INTO MANY UNIVERSITIES SO HE TOOK CLASSES AT A COMMUNITY COLLEGE.
COMMUNITY COLLEGE
A B A- B+
COMMUNITY COLLEGE HELPED NELSON BUILD THE CONFIDENCE AND SKILLS HE NEEDED TO TRANSFER INTO A UNIVERSITY.
UNIVERSITY

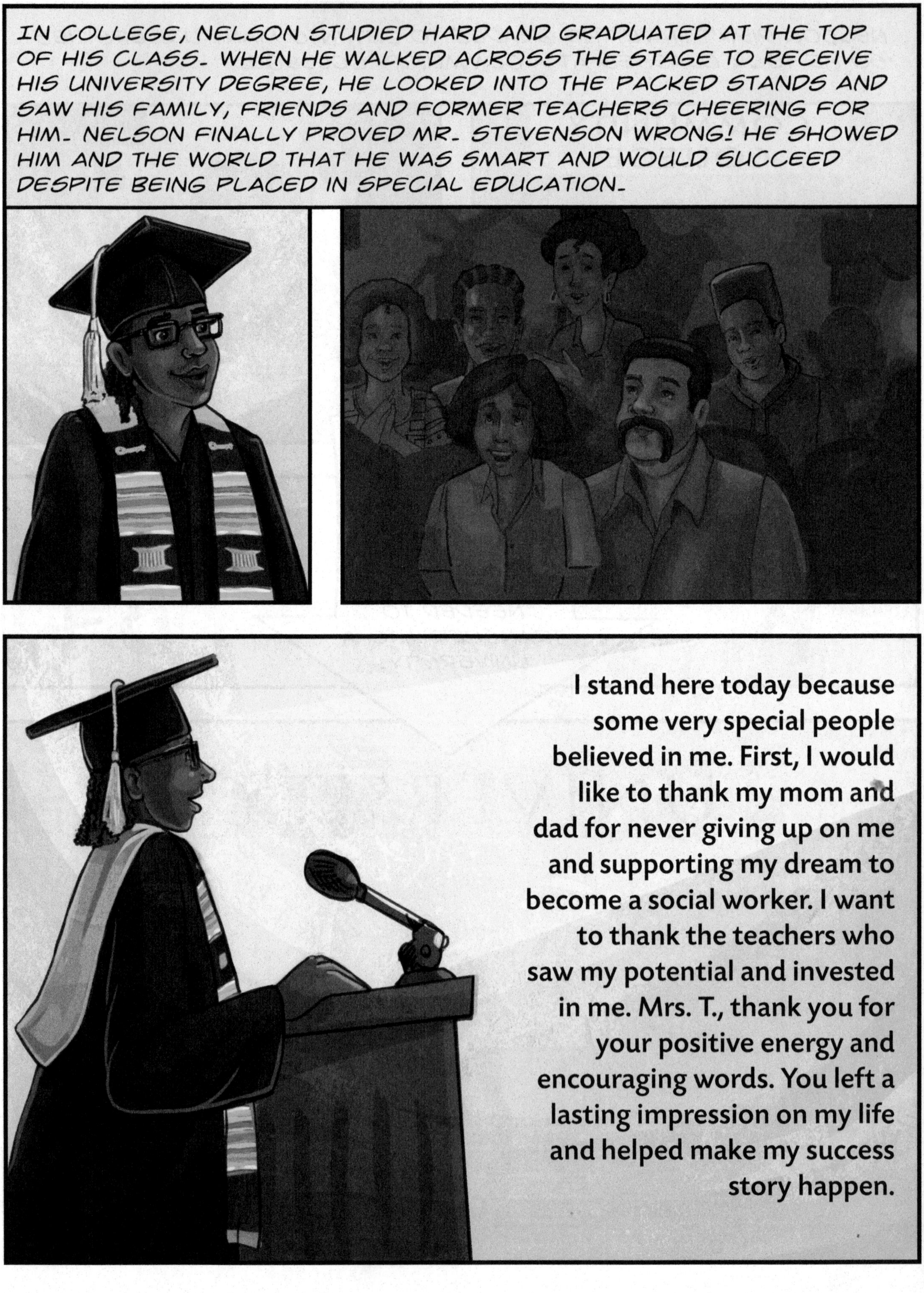
IN COLLEGE, NELSON STUDIED HARD AND GRADUATED AT THE TOP OF HIS CLASS. WHEN HE WALKED ACROSS THE STAGE TO RECEIVE HIS UNIVERSITY DEGREE, HE LOOKED INTO THE PACKED STANDS AND SAW HIS FAMILY, FRIENDS AND FORMER TEACHERS CHEERING FOR HIM. NELSON FINALLY PROVED MR. STEVENSON WRONG! HE SHOWED HIM AND THE WORLD THAT HE WAS SMART AND WOULD SUCCEED DESPITE BEING PLACED IN SPECIAL EDUCATION.
I stand here today because some very special people believed in me. First, I would like to thank my mom and dad for never giving up on me and supporting my dream to become a social worker. I want to thank the teachers who saw my potential and invested in me. Mrs. T., thank you for your positive energy and encouraging words. You left a lasting impression on my life and helped make my success story happen.

CPSIA information can be obtained
at www.ICGtesting.com
Printed in the USA
LVOW02*1512011216

515342LV00003B/48/P